Islamic Art Meets British Flowers

Born in Al-Yarmouk Refugee Camp south of Damascus, Syria, Hadil Tamim is proud of her lineage, deeply rooted in occupied Palestine. Due to the nature of her father's diplomatic position, Hadil lived in several countries and was exposed to a wide spectrum of cultures. While living in Ankara, Turkey, she obtained her professional degree in Ceramic and Islamic Decorative Art. She has been living in Reading, UK, together with her husband and two sons since 2000. In 2011 she obtained an academic foundation degree in Art in Practice from University of West London, UK.

After an eclectic career, part of which was spent looking after many of Reading's outdoor spaces, Adrian Lawson was extremely fortunate to be able to take early retirement with the intention of spending less time with his family. Since then he has been a bike mechanic, school bus driver, lorry driver trainer and campaigner for cycle facilities. Other than that, he spends his days teaching English to refugees and asylum seekers, walking his four dogs and birdwatching. He has a partner, Anne, three kids and a taste for loud and bizarre music.

Also published by Two Rivers Press

The Whole Story: Painting more than just the flowers by Christina Hart-Davies
The Art & History of Whiteknights edited by Jenny Halstead
The Art of Peter Hay by John Froy with Martin Andrews
Bonjour Mr Inshaw by Peter Robinson & David Inshaw
Botanical Artistry by Julia Trickey
The Greenwood Trees: History, folklore and uses of Britain's trees by Christina Hart-Davies
Reading Abbey and the Abbey Quarter by Peter Durrant and John Painter
Reading's Bayeux Tapestry by Reading Museum
A Coming of Age: Celebrating 18 Years of Botanical Painting by the Eden Project Florilegium Society
   by Ros Franklin
A Wild Plant Year: History, folklore and uses of Britain's flora by Christina Hart-Davies
Silchester: Life on the Dig by Jenny Halstead & Michael Fulford
Caught on Camera: Reading in the 70s by Terry Allsop
Plant Portraits by Post: Post & Go British Flora by Julia Trickey
Allen W. Seaby: Art and Nature by Martin Andrews & Robert Gillmor
Cover Birds by Robert Gillmor
An Artist's Year in the Harris Garden by Jenny Halstead
Caversham Court Gardens: A Heritage Guide by Friends of Caversham Court Gardens
Birds, Blocks & Stamps: Post & Go Birds of Britain by Robert Gillmor
Down by the River: The Thames and Kennet in Reading by Gillian Clark

Islamic Art Meets British Flowers

Hadil Tamim & Adrian Lawson

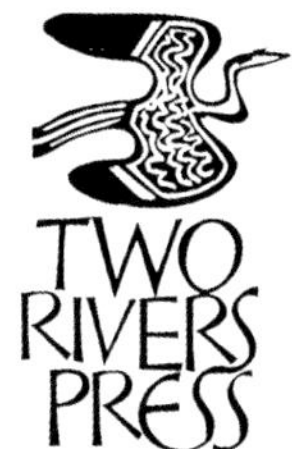

TWO
RIVERS
PRESS

First published in the UK in 2021 by Two Rivers Press
7 Denmark Road, Reading RG1 5PA
www.tworiverspress.com

ISBN 978-1-909747-45-6

1 2 3 4 5 6 7 8 9

Two Rivers Press is represented in the UK by Inpress Ltd and distributed
by Ingram Publisher Services UK.

Cover design by Nadja Guggi with an illustration by Hadil Tamim
Text design by Nadja Guggi and typeset in Parisine

Printed and bound in Great Britain by Gomer Press, Llandysul

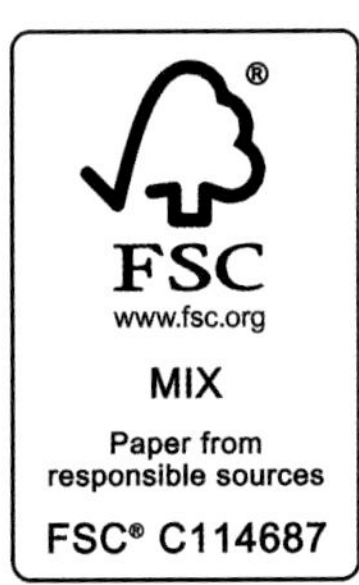

Acknowledgements

This book is a result of cooperation between two individuals with diverse backgrounds and expertise.

Hadil is grateful to her family and in particular, her husband Saleh, who provided support and help with language and editing. She also extends her gratitude to her parents, Kız Teknik Öğretim Olgunlaşma Enstitüsü, and the Ministry of Culture and Tourism of the Republic of Turkey, who provided her with her initial knowledge and training in Islamic decorative art. Special appreciation is also due to one of the most distinguished people in her life, her late tutor and mentor, Tezhip artist Ömer Faruk Atabek (1933–1999).

Two Rivers Press believed in the project from the start and helped bring it to fruition.

Special thanks to the Mahmoud Darwish Foundation for granting permission to include some of Darwish's beautiful poetic verse.

Picture credits (photography)

Suzanne Stallard: 2 (Adrian Lawson)

Mohammed Abdalla: 2 (Hadil Tamim)

Hadil Tamim: 8, 9, 11, 12, 13

Nadja Guggi: 19, 22

Adrian Lawson: 24, 44, 49

Sally Mortimore: 45

Contents

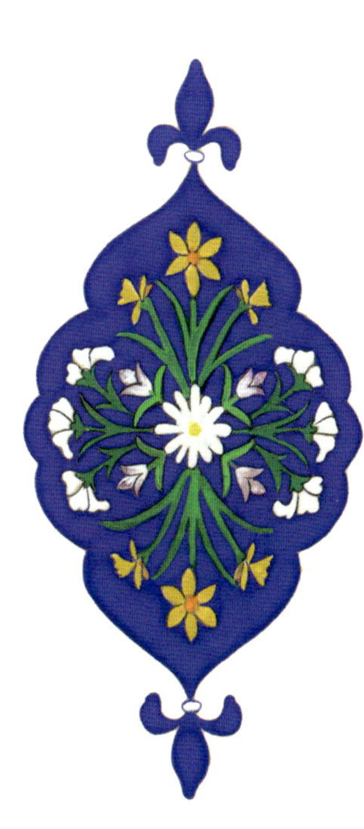

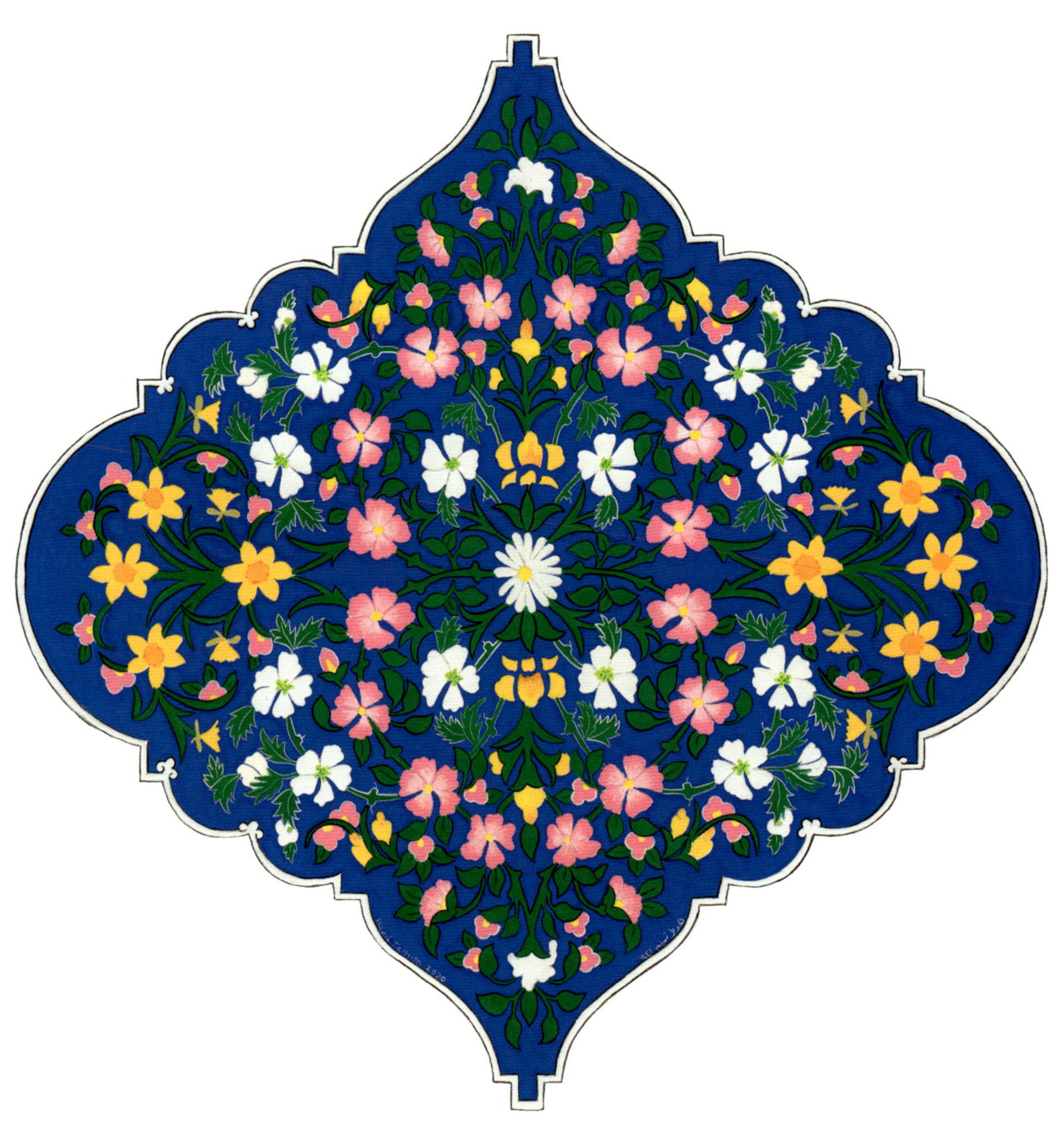

How the book came about

Hadil and Adrian met at the drop-in session at Reading Refugee Support Group. Every Monday, local people from the Reading area meet up with those who have come to the centre for support. Initially the objective was to help new arrivals learn conversational English, but now it is a place where people arrange to meet up, receive and offer help, chat, share news and/or just hang out.

Hadil's love of Reading has grown since she arrived here some 20 years ago, and her artist's eye was drawn to the brickwork and architectural forms of many of the buildings. She has always been inspired by nature and quickly noticed and identified the seasonal wildflowers she came across in the parks and open spaces.

Adrian came to Reading from London, where he grew up, and worked for Reading Borough Council looking after the town's open spaces for about 20 years. He is still active in improving the biodiversity of some of them in his spare time. Alongside his work, he penned a regular column in one of the local papers about the wildlife to be found in Reading and environs through the seasons and has published two books on the local trees and nature.

Neither Hadil nor Adrian came to Reading because of its flora and fauna but both have been riveted by its subtle but pervasive influence over them during their time here.

Their shared enthusiasm led to this collaboration. Hadil selected the flowers for their visual appeal, drawing many after extensive research in Fobney Island nature reserve, which Adrian was involved with from its start in the early 1990s. It was seeded with a wildflower meadow mix and thus enabled Hadil to study the flowers relatively easily.

Flowers have something in common with migration. Sometimes they escape the confines of a garden for life in a better place, sometimes arriving from a distant homeland and going on to do rather better

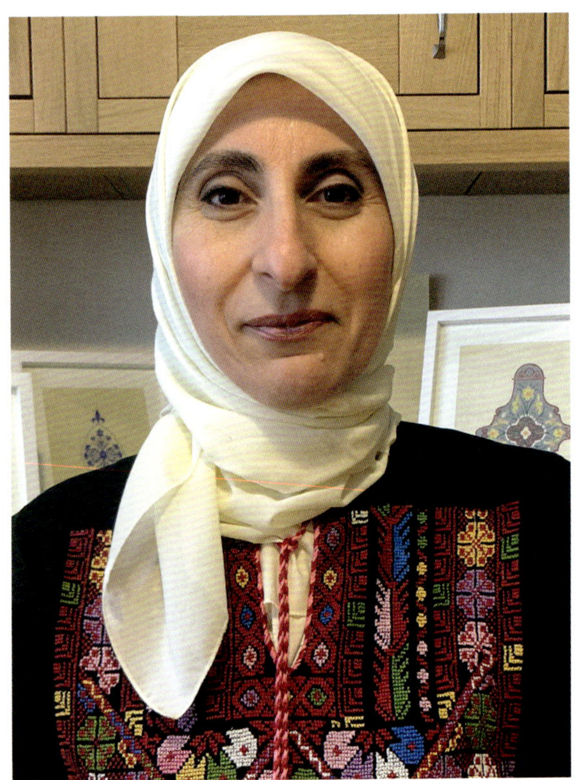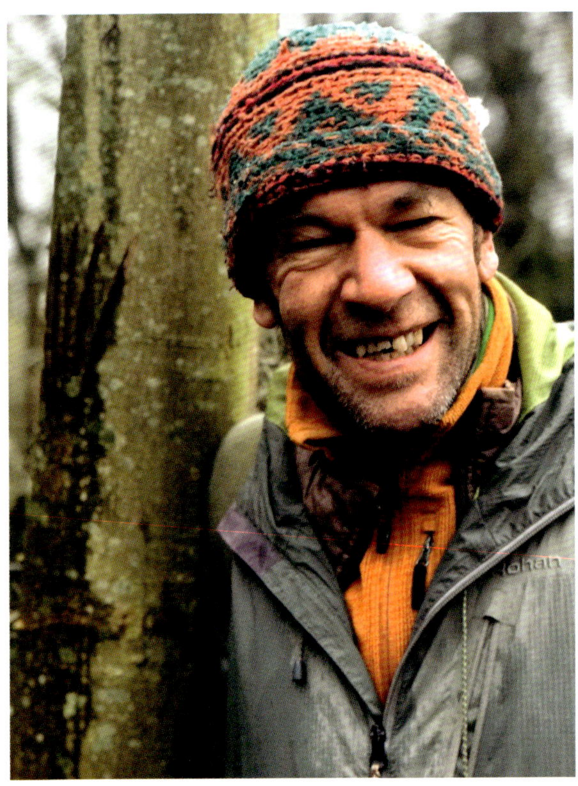

Hadil Tamim and Adrian Lawson

here. Others move from their original habitats because the conditions change – they dry out or become too shady. They reflect Reading, where people from all over the world settle and enrich the town, and form an apt metaphor for our times. Inhospitable environments, whether caused by human activities or climate change, cause people and flowers to move.

Introduction

BY HADIL TAMIM

A brief history of Islamic art

The term 'Islamic art' describes the art and architecture historically produced in the territories ruled by Muslims, produced for Muslim patrons, or created by Muslim artists. Although it is used to serve the Islamic religion, in mosque decoration for example, it is not strictly speaking a religious art.

Islamic art emerged from the disciplines and styles of previous civilisations like that of the Byzantines. The earliest Islamic art was mainly the work of 7th-century artists who had worked under Byzantine or Sasanian patronage and continued to use their own indigenous styles but for Muslim patrons, even before converting to Islam. They used their skills, techniques and expertise to create a wide range of styles.

With the wide geographical spread of Islam after the 7th century, broader and more diverse artistic styles joined in, which enriched the design, techniques and media (e.g. textiles, manuscripts, objects, and buildings) of the art. The earliest artforms displaying the unique features of Islamic art that had thus emerged appeared under the Umayyad Patronage (circa 660–750 AD). The Dome of the Rock in Jerusalem, which was the first major Umayyad architectural undertaking and completed in 691, is decorated with a mixture of Greco-Roman, Byzantine and Sasanian elements integrated harmoniously. The further spread of Islam during the subsequent eras of Abbasid (circa 750–1260 AD), Mongol (circa 1260–1330), Safavids (circa 1500–1720 AD), Ottomans (circa 1300–1920 AD) introduced even more richness as artistic styles were adopted from the newly conquered nations.

There are four basic elements of Islamic ornament, which may or may not occur together. They are:

- calligraphy
- plant-based motifs
- geometric motifs
- figural representations which depict nature and environment in an abstract way.

Since Islamic art reflects the cultural values of the Islamic world and reveals the way Muslims view the spiritual realm and the universe, artists explore a wide range of complex compositions based on these four basic elements. This book focuses on the use of the plant-based motifs.

Plant-based motifs and patterns appear in different forms and types from the earliest period of Islamic art and continue to be included in contemporary art in forms that make use of grids, repetition, reflection and freehand styles. This kind of motif was inspired by surrounding civilisations such as the Chinese and Persian so, originally, the main stylised plants were the lotus and the peony flower. The Ottoman era was characterised by using tulips, carnations and roses. The 16th century witnessed artists starting to incorporate realistic flowers and blossoms.

Illumination art (also known as Gilding art or Tezhip) is the use of radiant colours, including gold and silver, to illuminate calligraphy headings and manuscripts. Decorated letters, borders and figurative scenes, also called miniatures, are the main forms of illumination. One widely used type of illumination is the Shamsa, which means 'a little sun' (rosette) in Arabic. Shamsa, which is typically composed of plant-based and geometric motifs, is traditionally used as ornamentation for the first pages of books. It is also used to divide verses or sections of text and to decorate chapter openers. You can also find it carved or engraved on various surfaces like wood, leather and metals.

In the same way as the other arts, Islamic architecture emerged from the civilisations of the time including the Romans, the Sassanids and the

Byzantines. Buildings were decorated to enrich their aesthetic appearance using various media such as ceramic, wood, metalwork, stone, bricks, glass and plaster, various techniques such as mosaic and plastering, and a wide range of colours. Over the last 14 centuries, the capital of the Islamic world has moved several times and, sometimes, reached as far as the Iberian Peninsula. The result is a rich variety of architectural styles inspired by the existing culture and environment of each new capital location. The work and businesses of artists and craftsmen flourished in the new capitals and motivated trade between the Islamic world and Europe. Venice and Sicily played an important role as a bridge between the two cultures enabling the exchange of goods like luxurious carpets, silk, porcelain and glasswork, and as a result, artistic styles were also swapped. Textiles and pottery decorated with Islamic motifs were highly valued in Europe as the inscriptions and ornamentation were not related to any religion and did not offend Christian sensibilities. Islamic art motifs and techniques also influenced European arts and crafts. A good example of the impact of motifs is what is known as Western Arabesque and one of the most widely used techniques imported by the Europeans is bookbinding. Many of the 19th-century European artists, like William Morris, were inspired by Islamic art and used plant-based motifs in a wide range of forms.

The expansion of the modern European civilisation had an evident impact on architecture and art in the Islamic world. The late Ottoman era witnessed the construction of several major European-style buildings like the Dolmabahçe Palace in Istanbul and Western contemporary art continues to be widely accepted and used in the Islamic world.

The exchange of ideas and practices across cultures, civilisations and worlds is fundamental to the development of art. This book is a tiny but proud contribution towards that exchange.

Islamic art and this book

I took my first steps into the vast world of Islamic decorative art in Ankara, where I was living in the early 1990s and completed a degree in Ceramic and Islamic Decorative Art. The formal traditions of this art took me on a journey through the floral abstraction of the 14th to 17th centuries and inspired a wide range of artwork using various media including porcelain and card paper, which I displayed at various exhibitions, events and museums. Throughout this journey I was exposed to the wonderful art of Illumination (Tezhip) under the supervision of one of its masters, Ömer Faruk Atabek. A move to England gave me the opportunity to take a foundation degree in Art in Practice from West London University which gave extra lustre to this long experience and enriched it with contemporary techniques.

Wandering through the parks in and around Reading, where I live now, I couldn't help noticing that the wildflowers are quite different from those commonly used in Islamic art and it sparked the idea of merging them with the formal disciplines I was familiar with. My sense of pattern also made me very appreciative of the distinctive architecture of the Victorian brick buildings surrounding me in Reading. The elaborate roof lines and the colour of the terracotta bricks laid in detailed arrangements inspired me to fill sketch books with designs, abstractions, patterns and colours.

Many experiments later (some successful, some less so), I had abstracted 15 British wildflowers and harmonised them with the principles of illumination art. I used architectural features from Reading's buildings as framing elements, a unique notion in this discipline, whilst retaining Islamic art's core principles of symmetry, repetition and free-hand style. Each flower is embraced by its own frame in a distinctive composition.

I'm not stopping now! This new stage of my journey is both inspiring and rewarding. It bridges the gap between the culture I grew up in and the culture I now live in and gives me an opportunity to offer a gift of creativity in place of the conflict that so often separates the two.

Card paper preparation, composition creating & painting

Each of my designs is a three-stage journey full of passion, curiosity, determination and joy. The first two stages are surface preparation and composition and can be carried out in parallel or in sequence. They are the starting point of this journey. The final stage is the colouring.

Surface preparation

Paper selection and paper-making

Ready-made 300 gsm ivory-coloured card is a practical choice of medium for illumination art and used for the designs in this book. An alternative is home-made (recycled) paper, which can be prepared as follows:

- shred newspaper and scrap paper
- soak the shredded paper in hot water for one or more days
- blend the mixture using a food processor to a smooth consistent pulp
- spread the paper pulp on a screen to dry.

Although the end result is almost three-dimensional thanks to the texture of the home-made paper, it is hard to apply colour to it in a consistent way. Therefore, using home-made paper requires extra care when applying the paints.

Staining the paper

It is traditional to dye paper surfaces before drawing. Although this is not strictly necessary, it gives the surface an antiquated appearance and adds to the depth and richness of the painting. Natural pigments, which have been used by artists all over the world for thousands of years, are still the choice of many artists nowadays as they're environmentally friendly and usually easier to manipulate, with sometimes surprising results. Coffee,

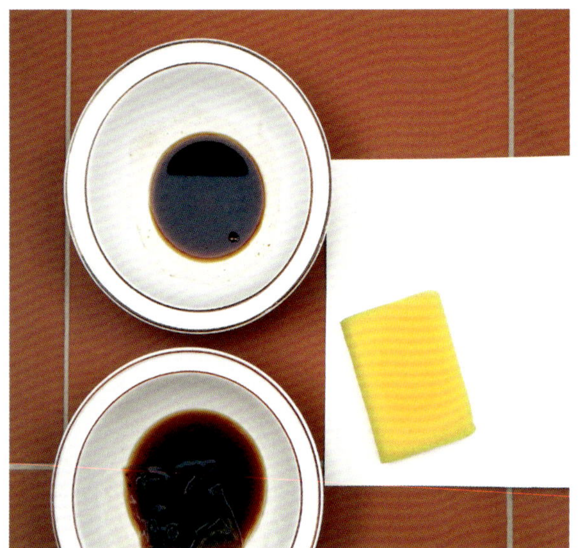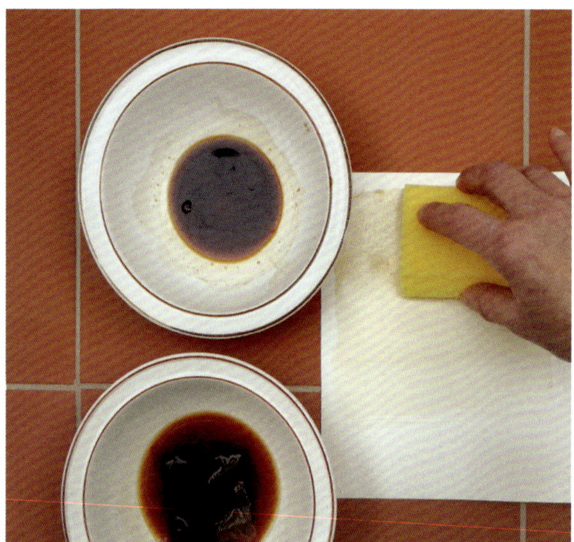

Coffee, tea and sage make a natural dye which I apply to the paper using a sponge, to create an antiquated look and add depth and richness to my paintings.

tea, flower petals, herbs, onion skin, pomegranate and green walnut peel are commonly used. The designs in this book were drawn on paper stained using coffee, tea and sage. Inspired by the famous Palestinian poet Mahmoud Darwish's poem 'Don't Apologise for What You Have Done', sage and thyme are the ingredients that provide Hadil with a spiritual connection to her homeland, Palestine.

The dye is prepared by either boiling the pigments or soaking them in boiling water for a period of time long enough to achieve the required colour gradient. A sponge or wide, smooth brush is used to apply the dye to the surface of the paper. This ensures even coverage over the whole surface. Applying a subsequent dye layer will create a darker paper but each layer should be completely dry before applying the next.

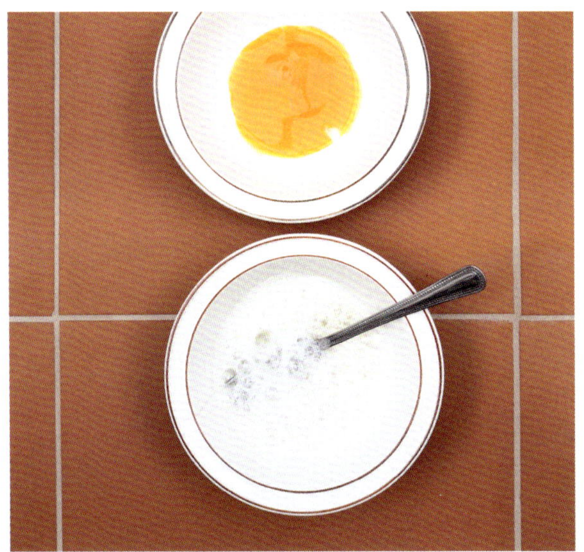 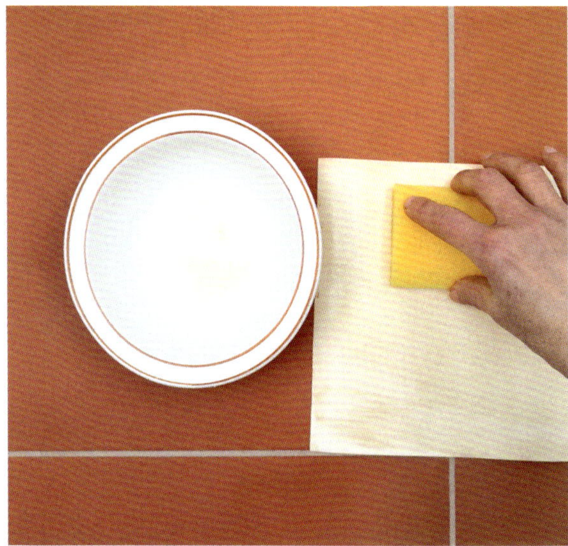

I use glair, the run-off from beaten egg whites, to coat the surface of the artwork and create a smooth surface ready for painting.

Glair

The glair technique is used to create a smooth, shiny and polished paper surface. Egg whites are beaten into a fluffy meringue and water sprinkled on the surface. The meringue is left to rest in the fridge for 24 hours resulting in a clear liquid forming beneath the fluff. This liquid is applied to the surface of the paper in the same way as the stain described earlier. A thicker coating is achieved by mixing some starch with water and applying it to the paper before applying the glair. Again, layers can be built up but sufficient time should be allowed for each coat to dry thoroughly before applying the next one.

The water in both dye and glair solutions causes buckling and curling in the paper. To eliminate this, the paper is placed on a rigid, smooth surface. Several heavy books or similar are placed on top of the paper and left for at least a week. The result is a paper with a shiny surface that will make the painting process smoother.

Composition

Composition design is a challenging stage full of research, exploration, experimentation and discovery. The composition should stick to the traditional design rules but must be original and unique. A lot of research on each of the various elements of the design is carried out. Sketching them in various ways and experimenting with different arrangements are some examples of the effort that is made to guarantee the harmony and the aesthetic appeal of the final product. There are always surprises along the way!

Each artwork in this book started with an observation that sparked an idea and developed into a theme. This was followed by exploring the environment in which the wildflower was found, taking notes on its growth habit, and taking photographs. This research required several visits

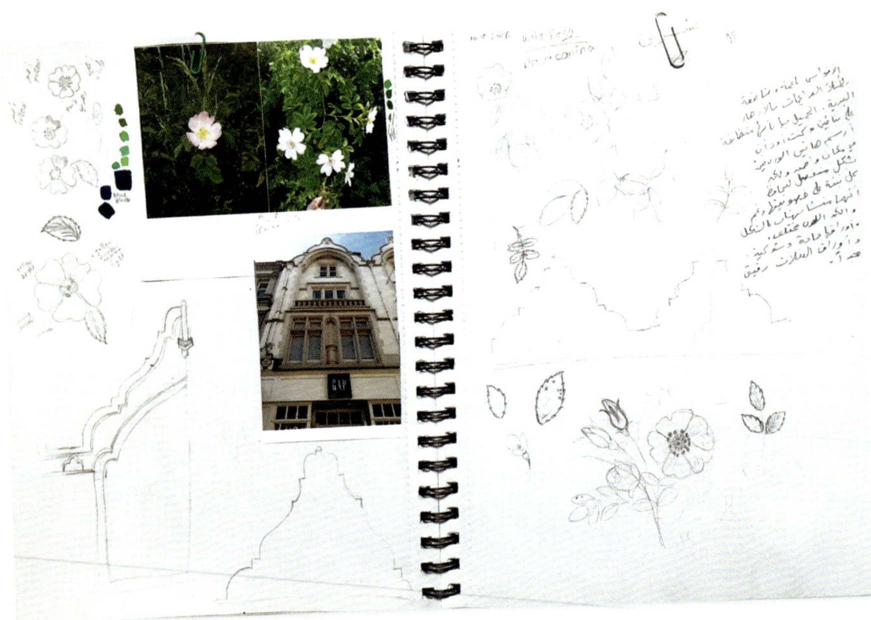

I use scrap paper to protect
the stained paper and create
a working space for my design,
which I sketch onto tracing paper
before transferring it to the
stained paper.

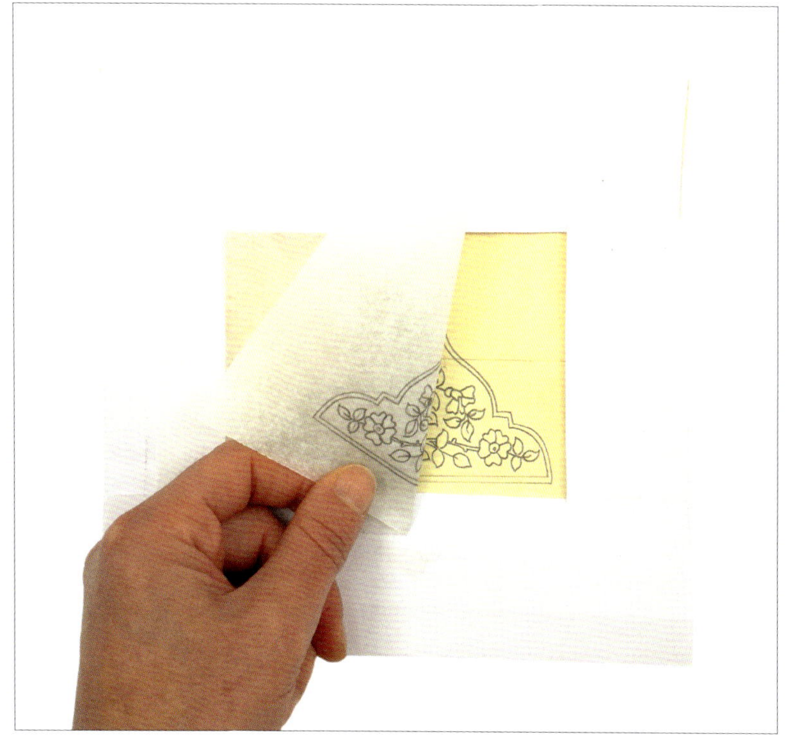

to the site. Each flower was then matched with an architectural feature of Reading taken from an already prepared archive containing features that had been discovered, photographed and documented earlier. The matching process is not straightforward as it requires several sketching trials to get to the final design.

First, a scrap paper frame is positioned over the stained paper to protect the edges and to provide a working space. The design is sketched onto tracing paper, which is glued onto the working frame. The design is then transferred onto the stained paper using a sharp pencil or pen.

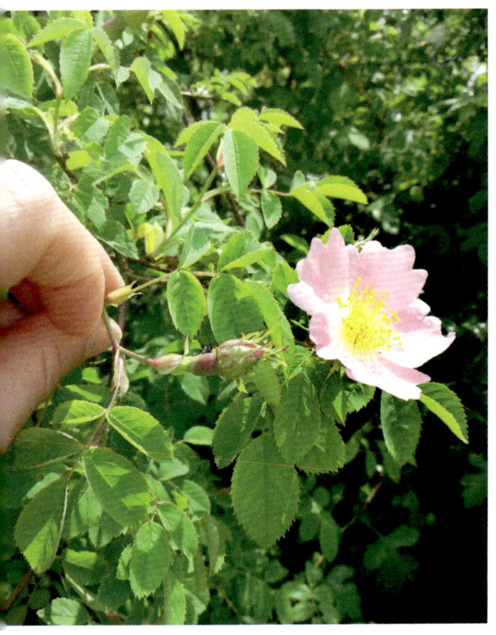

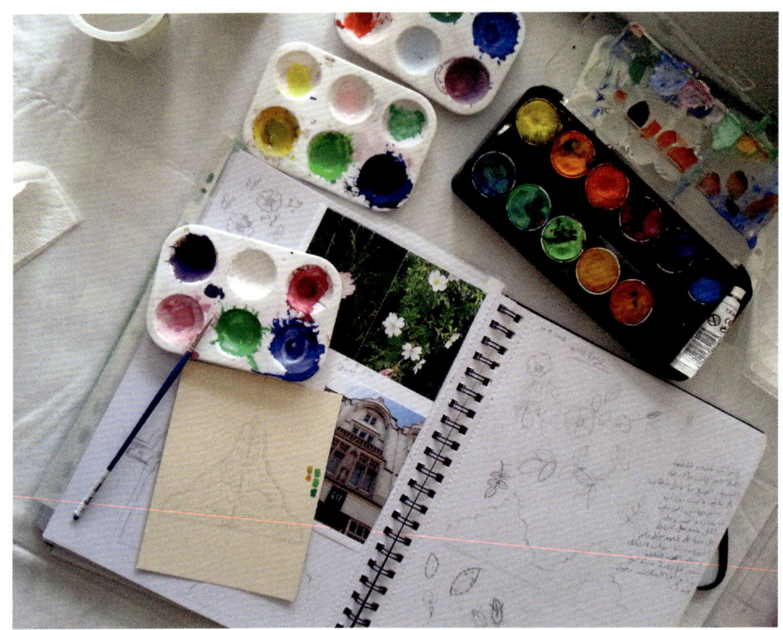

Colour

Colour palette

Colour preparation is a fundamental stage in the painting process because it needs to accurately reflect the final vision for the artwork.

First, the relevant colour palette is created. This includes experimenting with various elements of the design independently to ensure they accurately reflect the natural forms that inspired them, before experimenting with various colour combinations to achieve the right balance.

Colouring in

The starting point is always the background of the floral composition before working on the leaves and flowers and, finally, the fine details. It's important to add just the right amount of water to the pigment to get

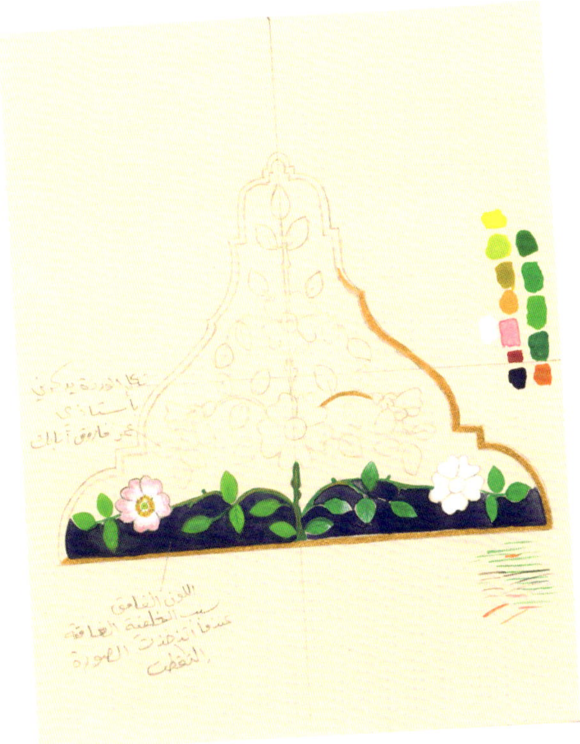

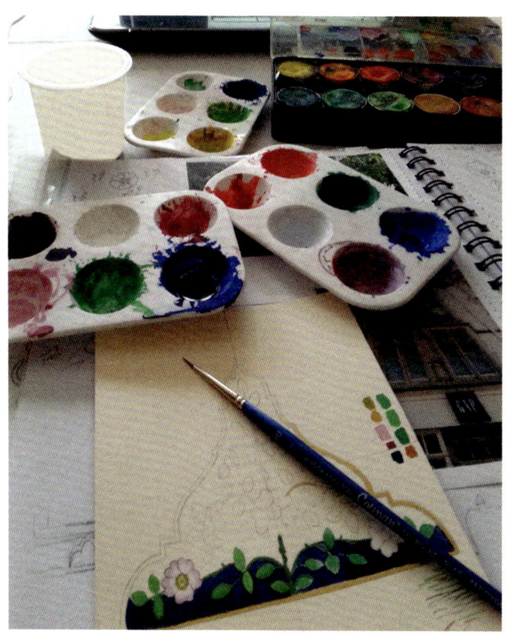

Experimentation with various colours and techniques usually leaves my working surface cluttered with pallets, brushes, notes, sketches, photos, etc. the right balance between fluidity and viscosity. Effort and time spent experimenting and testing the colour before applying it are never wasted. Holding the paint brush vertically helps to control the rate of flow of the paint from the brush to the paper.

Here is an excerpt from Hadil's sketchbook to show examples of her experimentation with colours. The shape of the central flower in this piece recalls the memory of the late Ömer Faruk Atabek (1933–1999), Hadil's tutor of illumination art techniques (Tezhip).

It's all about experimentation
and surprise. I start with
an abstract idea which needs
developing and maturing.
Days of experiments do that.
Sometimes the final result
is unexpected.

Snowdrop

Galanthus nivalis

زهرة الثلج

Flowers are very symbolic for many reasons, and none more so than the common snowdrop, which is especially adapted to pierce through snow and has long had an association with purity. The flowers appear in mid-winter, with the lengthening days and shortening shadows. At a time when daylight is limited and our mood can be at a low ebb, to spot a snowdrop, or better still a carpet of them, can really lift the spirits.

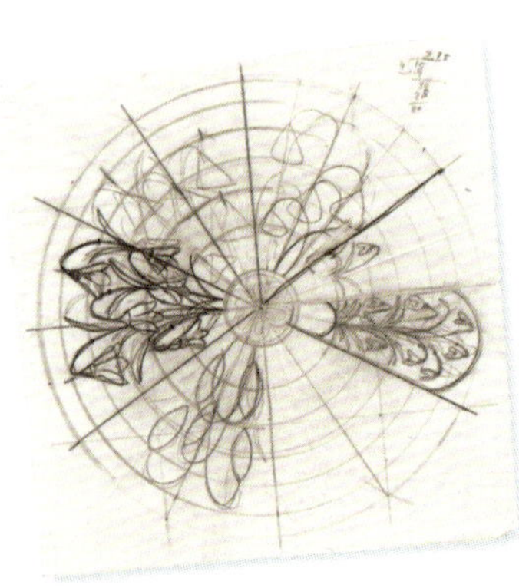

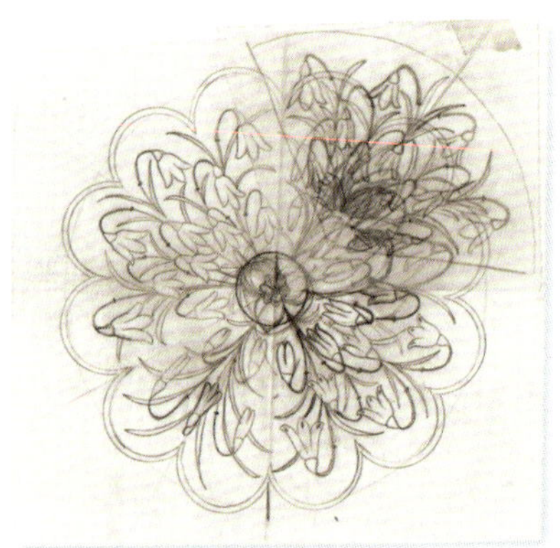

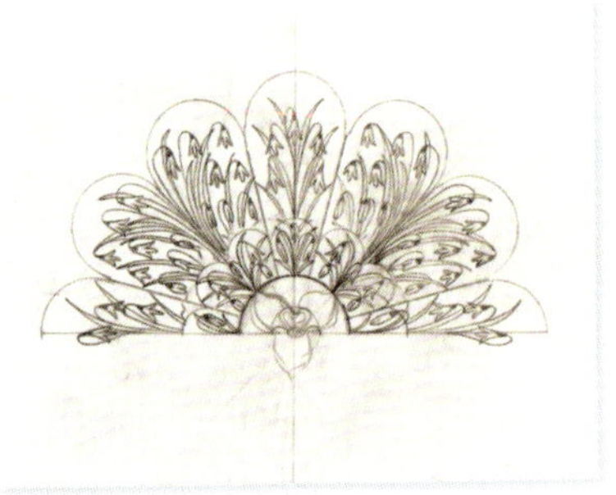

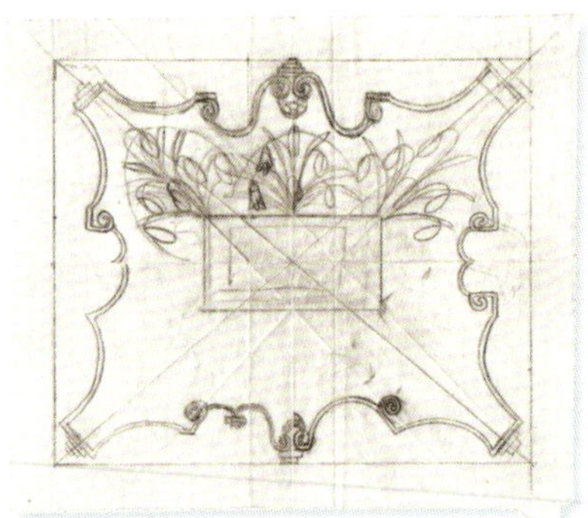

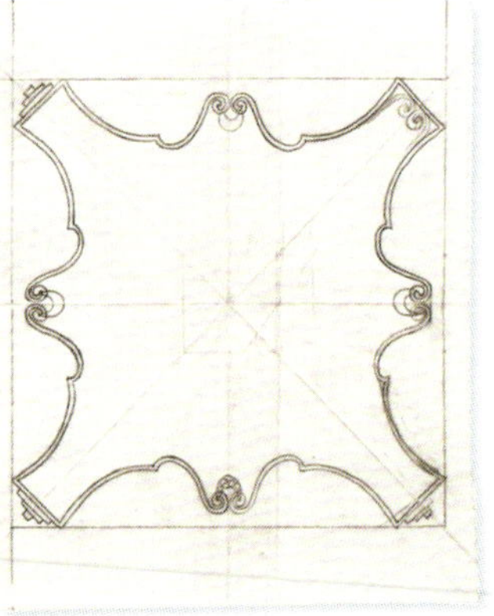

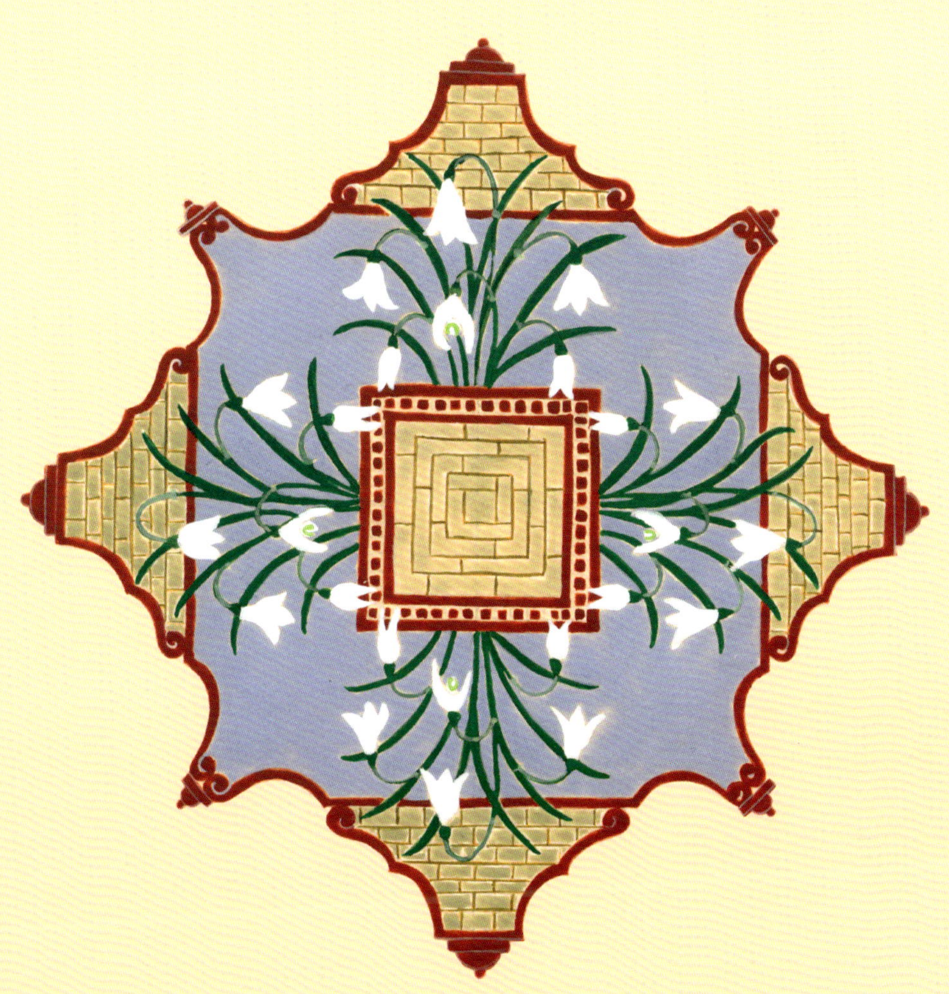

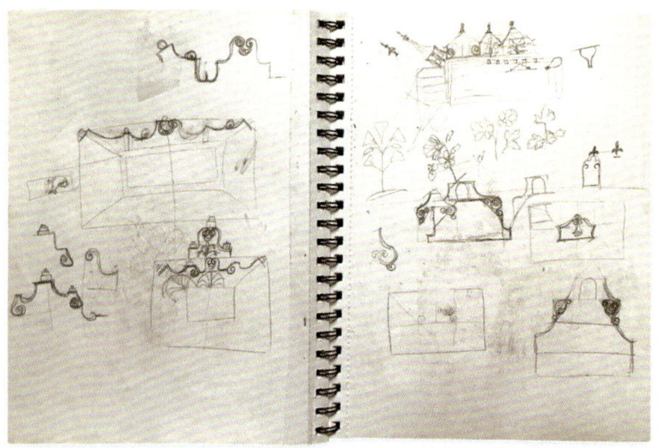

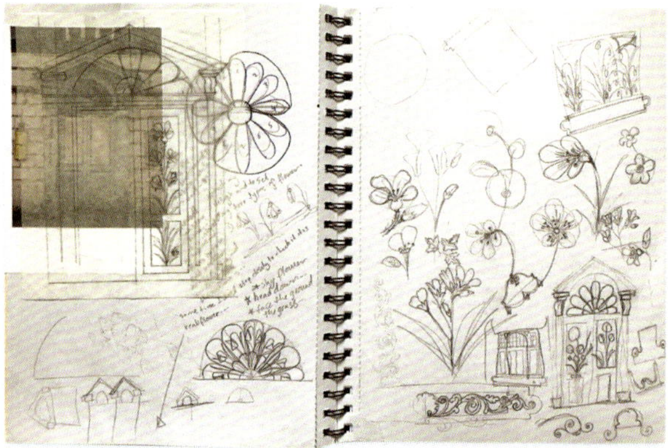

The flowers flourish during February and have vanished by April, but their short-lived season is one to be cherished as it signifies that spring, many people's favourite season, is not so far away.

They like damp shady places and exhibit an air of wildness, sprouting in myriad out-of-the-way places. Once established they can outlive human settlements and provide clues to the past. For example, a large clump of snowdrops grows in a wet woodland where a cottage once stood.

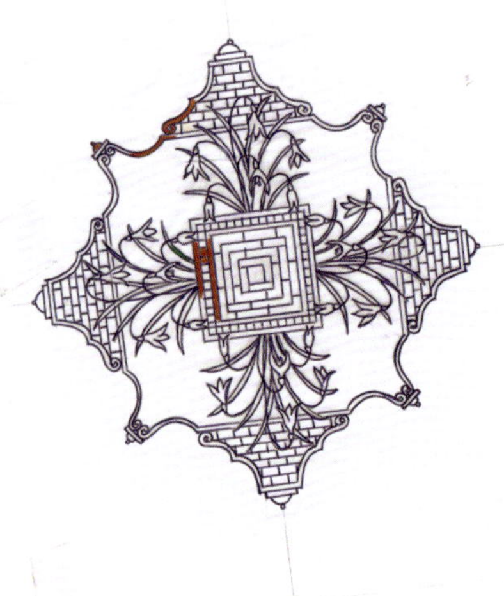

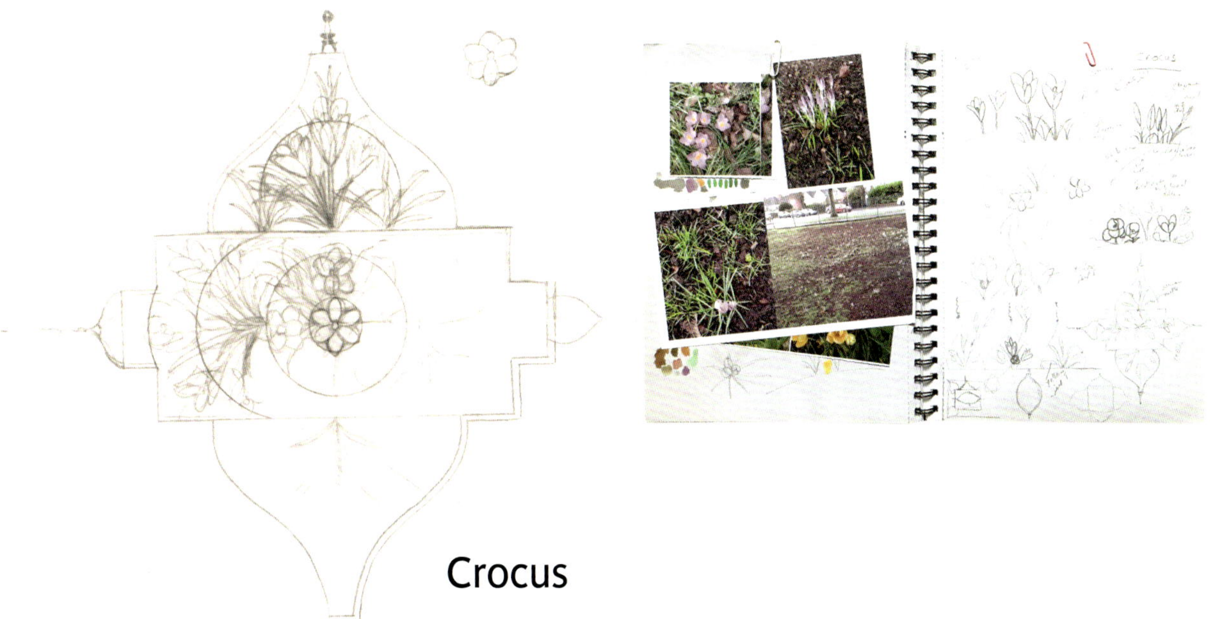

Crocus

Crocus spp.

زعفران

There are many species of crocus in the grass verges, parks and gardens of towns. They are one of the most widely planted corms and appear early in the year, flowering from mid-January to late March. They are a cheap and effective way to brighten up grass verges and they revive many municipal flower beds during winter. Churchyards often contain colourful displays, which remind you that the soil really is still alive in winter, and soon the ground will be lush and green once more.

As they flower and then fade away before the grass starts to grow, they do very well in lawns before the mowers come out, although they almost never get the chance to set seed. If mowing is delayed, the seed heads emerge, curious pods on stalks, and if left long enough they can set ripe seed and naturalise. Sadly, grey squirrels often dig up the corms in winter and if they get into the habit whole displays can suddenly vanish.

The different species come in many colours: pale, fragile mauves; rich, egg-yolk yellow; snow white; and deep purple.

Early spring brings new life. Although it looks otherwise, soil stays alive in winter. The ground is lush and green once more. The crocus is one of the first flowers to blossom.

Opposite page:
More experimentation and more surprises.

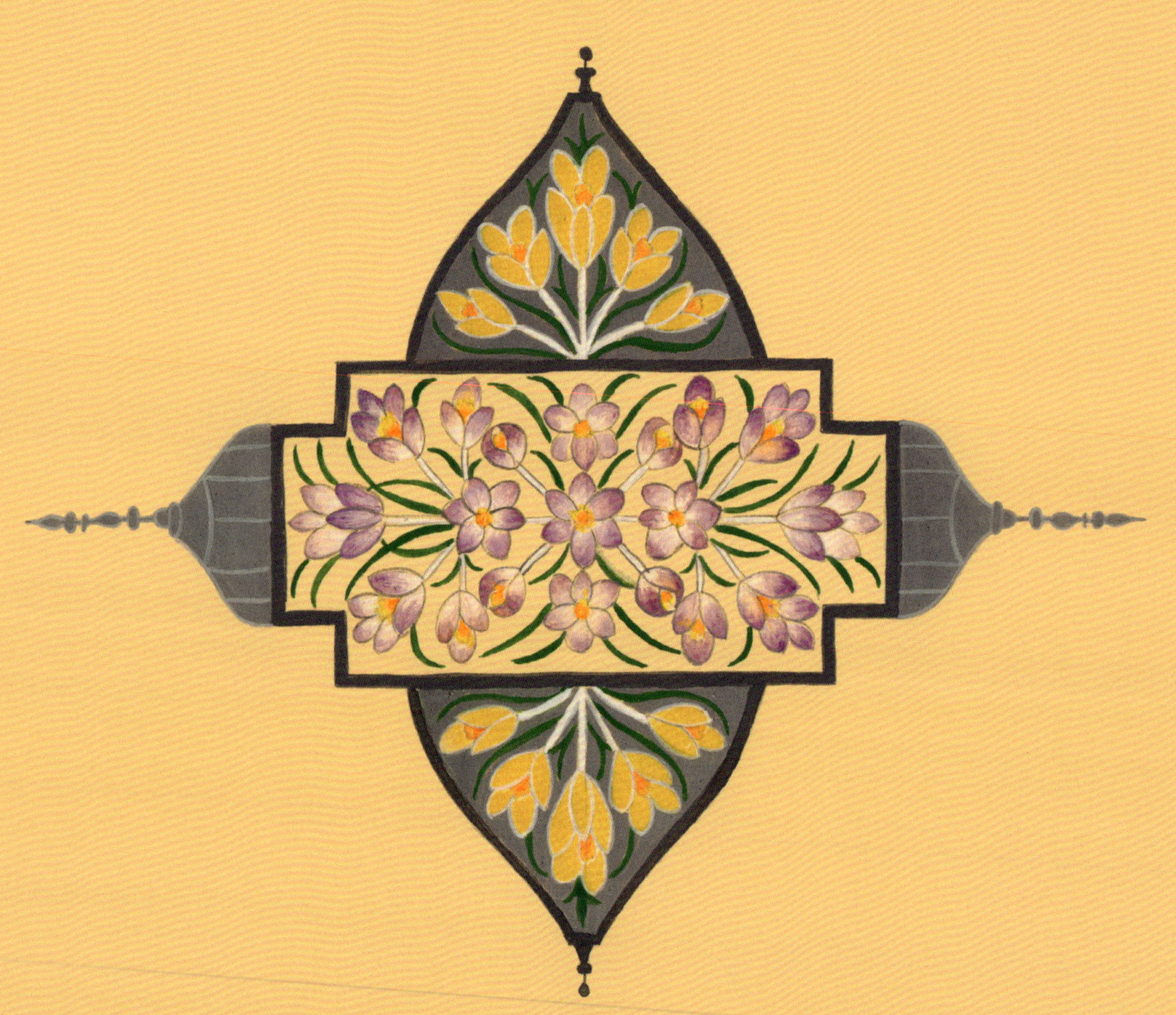

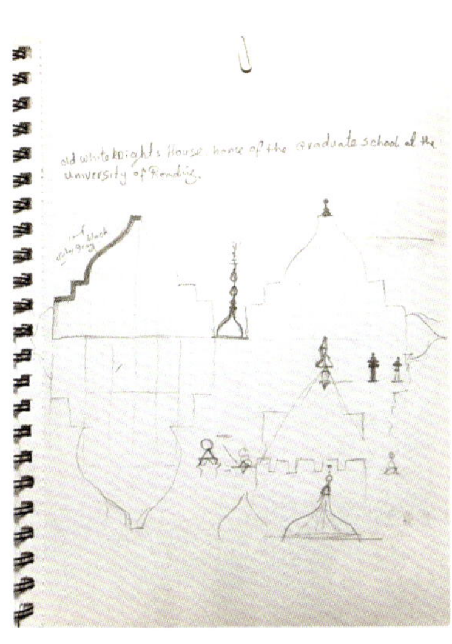

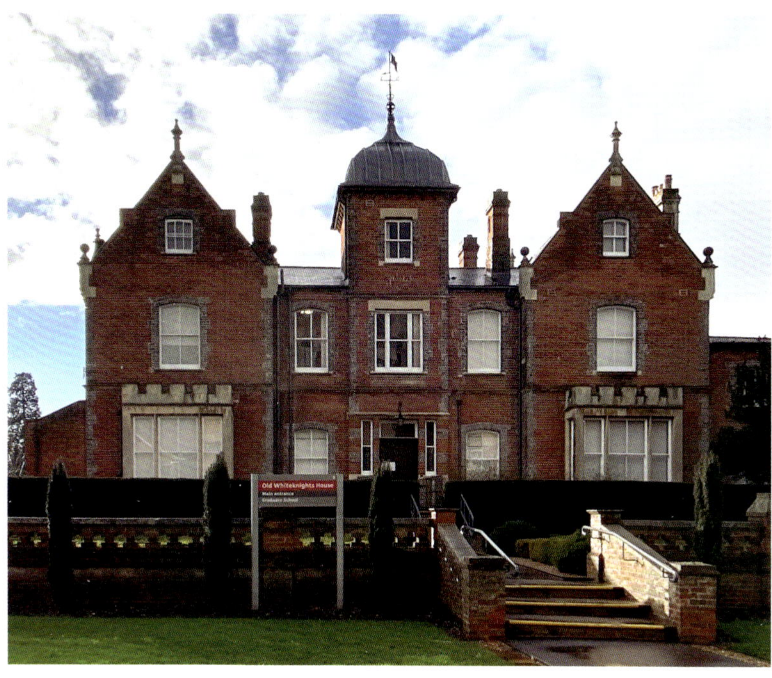

Crocus flowers with their beautiful colours are combined with the distinctive grey domes of Old Whiteknights House.

On a warm day the early white-tailed bumble bee is a regular visitor for some early nectar. House sparrows are attracted to the yellow species but the decline in their populations means the flowers survive undamaged more often in recent years.

The crocus painting features mauve and yellow crocuses, which are abundant in the lawns of Reading University and the picture frame mirrors the outline of Old Whiteknights House on the campus. This charming building with its grey dome and distinctive arches is currently home to the Graduate Schools of Arts & Humanities and Social Sciences and was designed by Alfred Waterhouse for his father. Waterhouse is responsible for many of Reading's iconic buildings including the Town Hall and Reading School, and also the Natural History Museum in London and Holborn Bars in Camden.

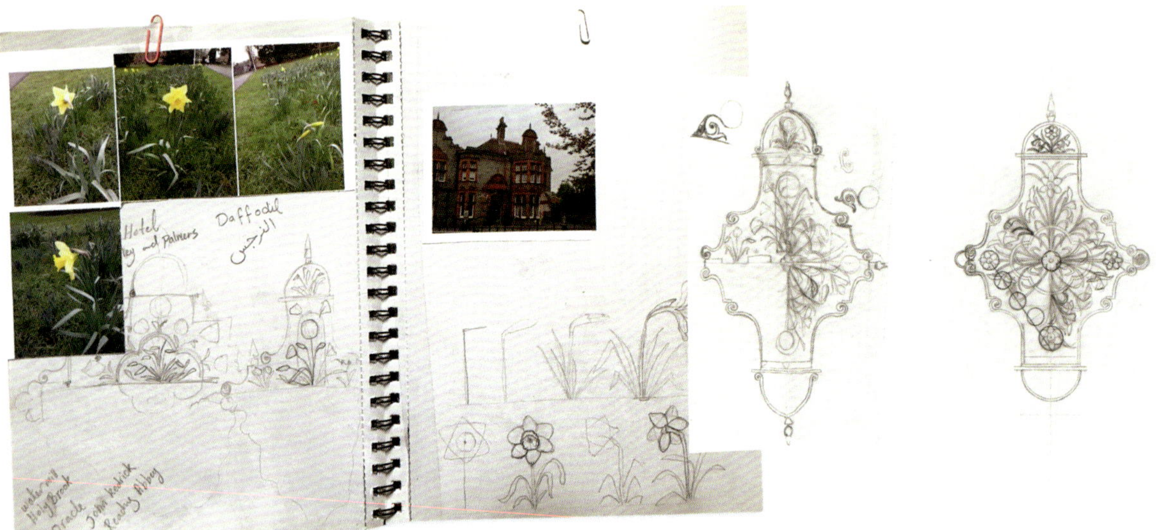

Daffodil

النرجس البري

Narcissus pseudonarcissus

It's almost impossible to think of daffodils as wildflowers anymore. Nowadays they are cultivated, bulbs are sold by the sackful and for a few short weeks in late winter they are just about everywhere, brightening up the winter landscape from late February to April.

Verges and parks across Britain have had a lot of money spent on them as councils have planted thousands of daffodils in them, producing spectacularly large flowering displays. They are rarely found in the wild but garden escapees that have made a bid for freedom sometimes form small clumps in woods and meadows. The real wild daffodil is a small, open flower and, although once incredibly common, is now very hard to find. The truly wild populations are now visitor attractions, such as those that grace The Daffodil Way around the Gloucestershire villages of Newent and Dymock.

Daffodil, with its bright yellow colour, brings positivity and hope, signalling the end of winter. It represents the richness of life emerging from the grass, and sometimes the snow.

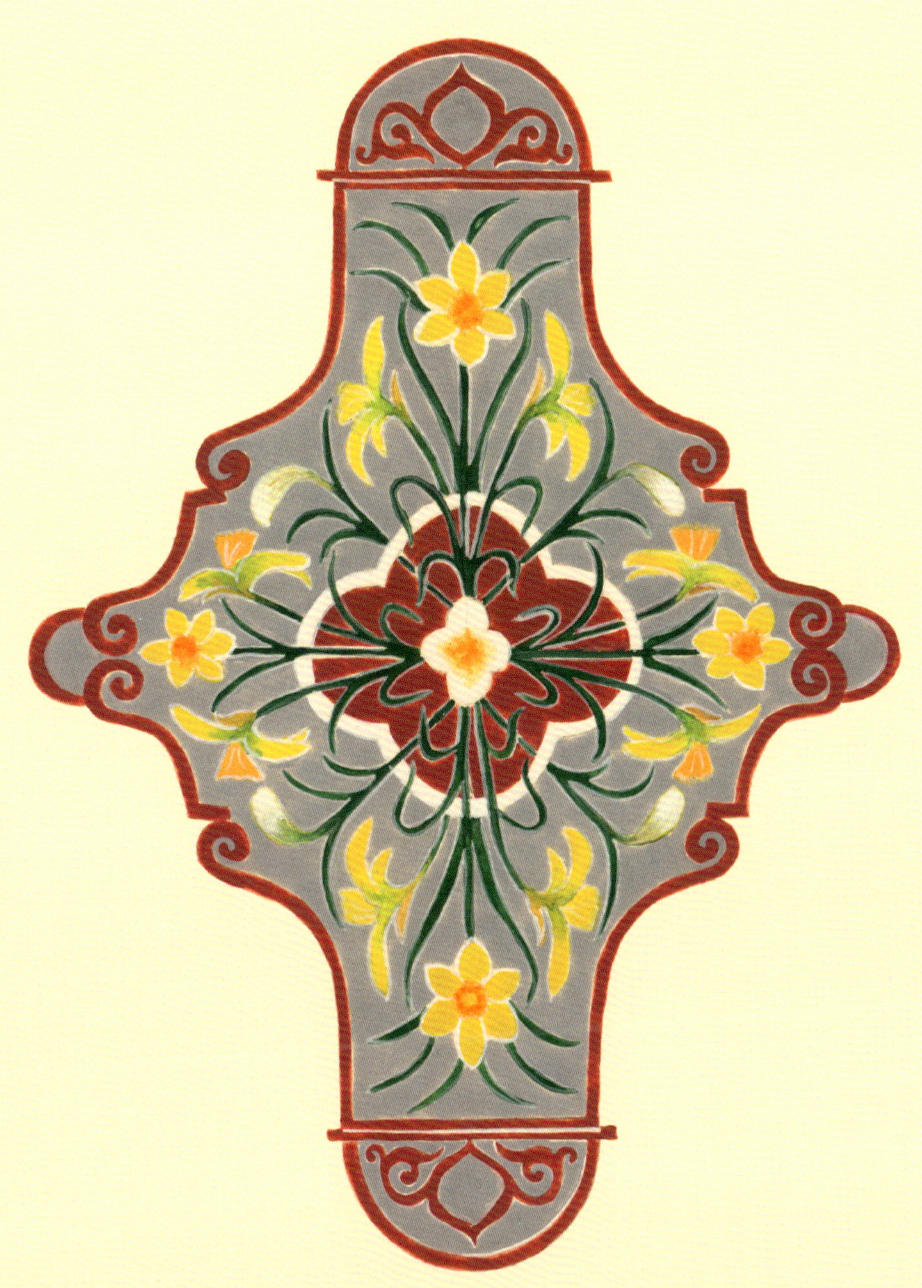

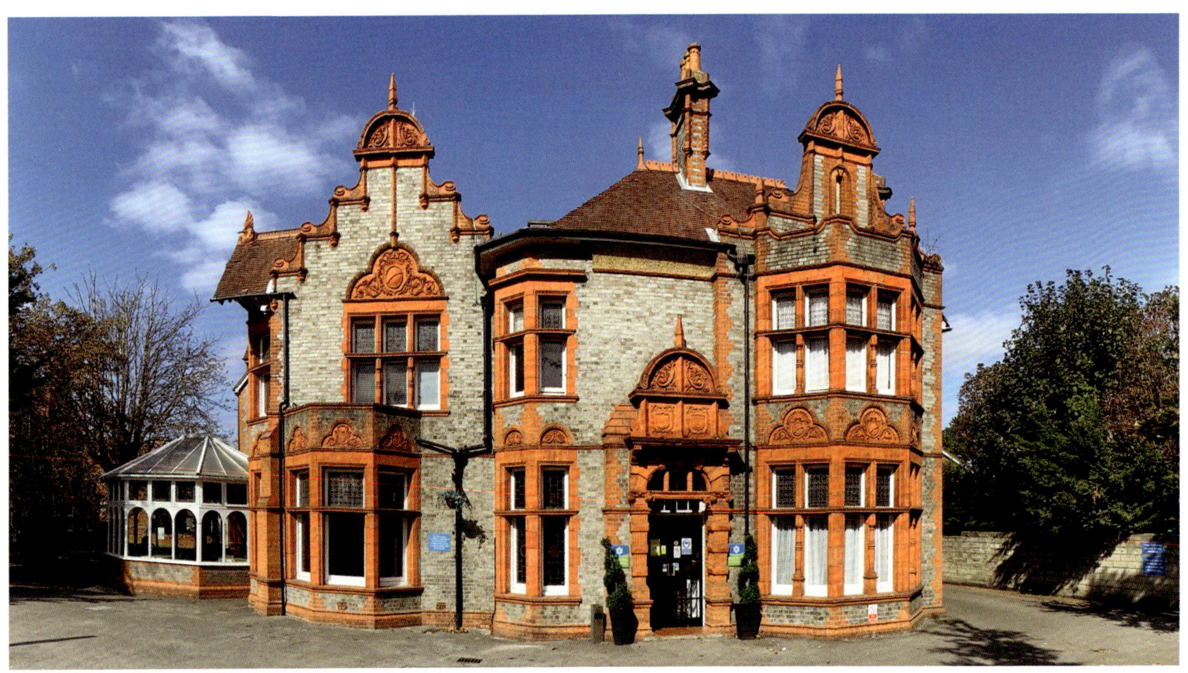

The unique architecture of Sure Hotel, with its decorative grey brick and deep red terracotta, was selected to embrace the daffodils.

The amazing variety in colour, size and form is derived from years of horticultural selection. The variety also extends the growing season so large-scale plantings can contain a broad palette of long-lasting flowers.

The frame for the daffodils is based on the former Hillingdon Prince hotel on Christchurch Road (now the Sure hotel by Best Western). The ornate decorative brickwork was a showcase for the brickmaker William Poulton, and the clay was from local kilns. The combination of grey brick with the deep red terracotta is used to great effect in this building and the number of decorative effects achieved with curves, steps, arches and motifs is impressive.

Lady's smock or Cuckoo flower

Cardamine pratensis الحُرف المرجي

A true wildflower that makes a significant impact when it flowers from mid-April through May. Most of the year, lady's smock is an unobtrusive little rosette in the grass, but in April the narrow stems reach up beyond the blades to show off their superbly delicate little clusters of very pale pink or nearly mauve flowers, nodding in the breeze.

Lady's smock is the better name. 'Cuckoo flower' is also used to describe many plants whose flowering is supposed to chime with the cuckoo's arrival in Britain after overwintering in Africa, but they flower usually well before the bird gets here. Perhaps the timings for either or both species were different in the past.

There are also many local names: 'milkmaids' is a common one; and 'fairy flower' aptly describes its delicate presence in the grass. It is related to the bittercresses (wavy and hairy), which are very common little urban weeds.

They like damp and short-grassed areas. They were massively affected by the drainage and use of fertilisers in meadows. As the soil dried out and the fertiliser took effect, the grass grew lush to feed cattle and smothered most of the wildflowers. Milkmaids were one of the victims. As some grasslands have started to recover from this damage the flowers have slowly come back. They hung on along riverbanks and streams and now flower all over the grazed Coley meadows and the managed conservation grassland of the Thames parks. Sadly, as milder winters start to dominate British weather, grasses get going earlier in the year and these flowers are often victims of over-efficient mowing just as they emerge. Hopefully, enlightened grass management regimes, or perhaps extensive flooding, will see a resurgence.

Like the snowdrop, the frame for this painting is inspired by the roofline of the front of the John Lewis store in Reading, which attracted Hadil's attention when she first visited the town centre in 2000. The

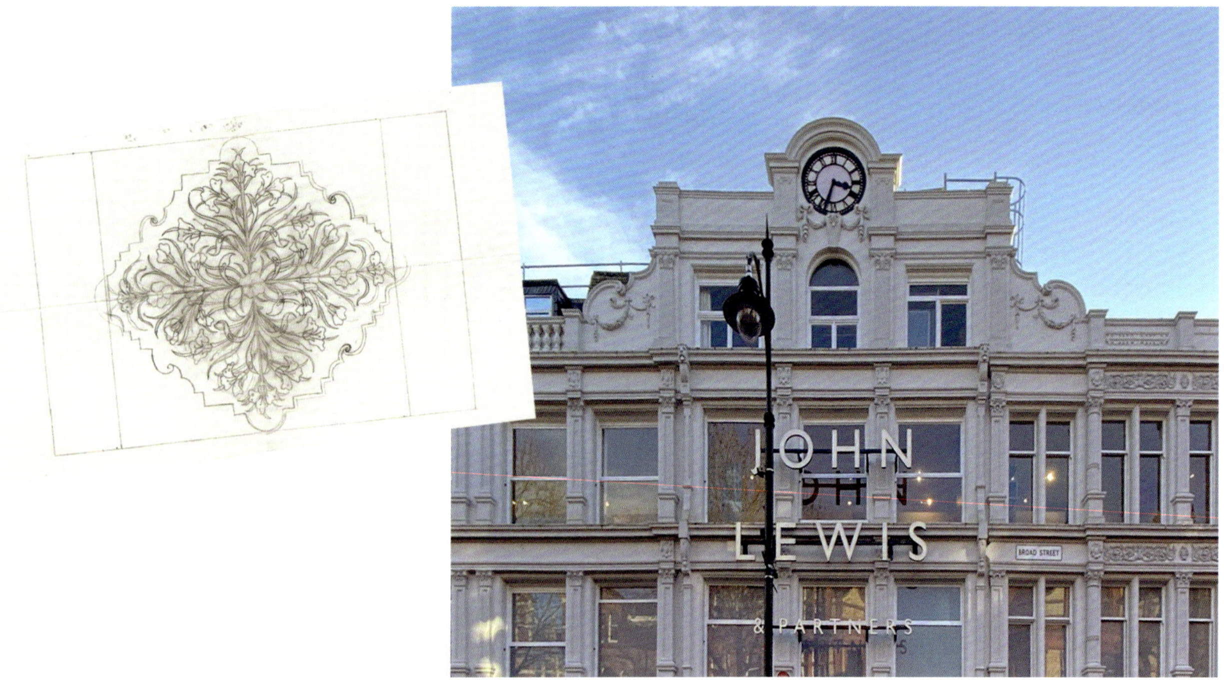

The roofline arch encircling the clock and the surrounding architectural elements on the front of the John Lewis store inspired the frame for the cuckoo flower composition. The first step of the experimentation journey is also shown.

iconic building, known to older Reading residents as the Heelas building, dominates Broad Street and is best approached from Queen Victoria Street in the north to appreciate the perspective. The part of the building depicted dates from 1907 when it was built as an extension of a shop in Minster street. It was at one time the largest shop in Berkshire. The whole site was redeveloped and reopened behind the old frontage in 1985.

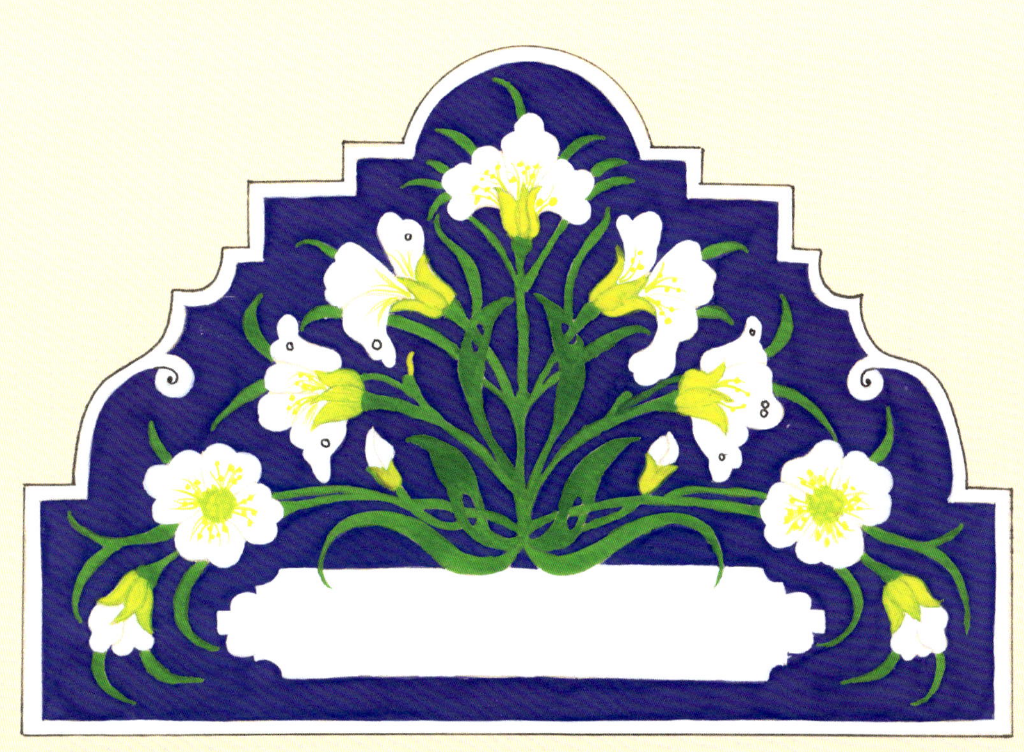

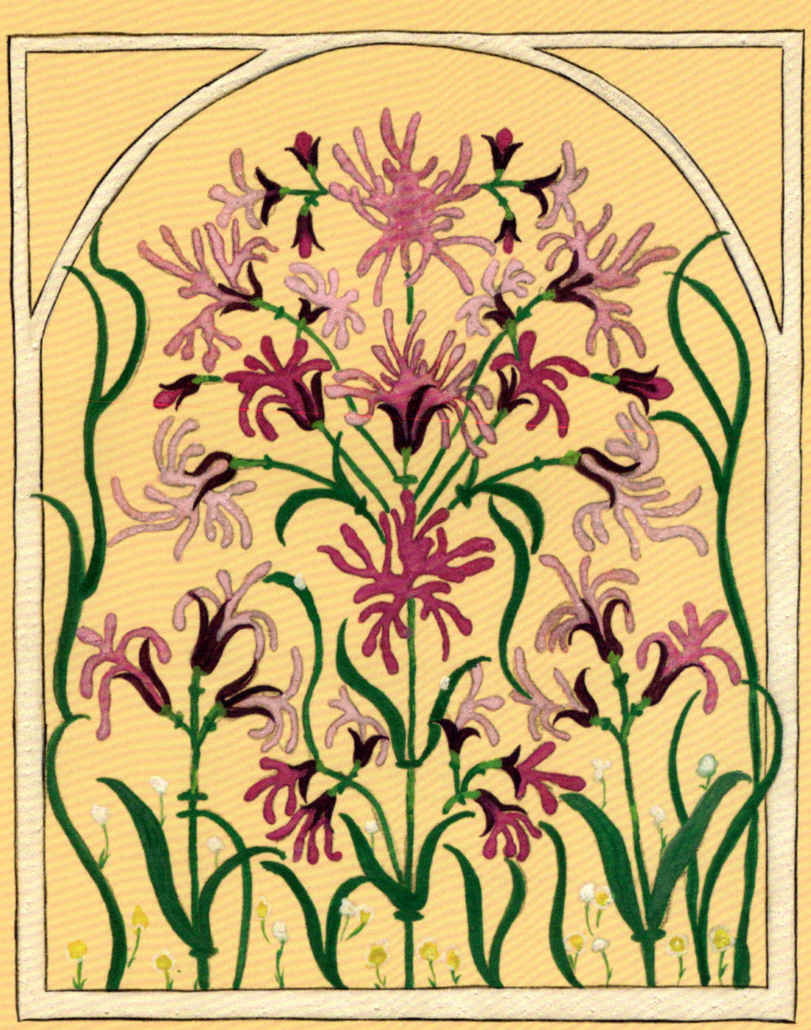

Ragged Robin

Lychnis flos-cuculi اللخنيس

Here is another spring-flowering plant (late May to early July) of damp meadows that's associated with the cuckoo – just like lady's smock. The Latin name *cuculi* refers to cuckoo.

The dark pink flowers are, as the name implies, ragged. Much like lady's smock, whose habitat they share, they have suffered a catastrophic decline but don't seem to be recovering half so well. The best place to see them around Reading is Fobney Island nature reserve, where they were part of the seed mix sown there when the reserve was created in 2012. Seed was also successfully sown around the northern foot of Christchurch bridge in Christchurch meadow as part of the construction and it seems to be doing well. In other places, look for them in damp meadows that have not been spoilt, or grasslands where they have been deliberately reintroduced. They should thrive there as long as the grass cutting regime is favourable.

Grass management must be done carefully to enable wildflower seeds to ripen and disperse so the next generation lands in just the right conditions for it to germinate and grow. In the past, meadows were cut later in the season and then, once the grass had dried, it was raked up and used as hay. There were plenty of opportunities for the dried pods to spill their seed in appropriate conditions to flower in the future. This traditional form of management took place all over lowland Britain for hundreds of years, which made so many of our wildflowers relatively common. The change in agricultural management, cutting grass earlier to produce silage and applying fertilisers, has wiped out this and many other abundant and beautiful flowers over vast areas. It is now very scarce locally.

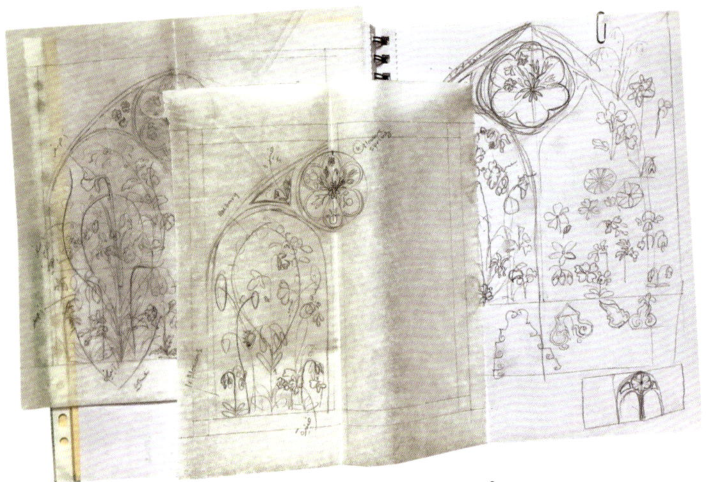

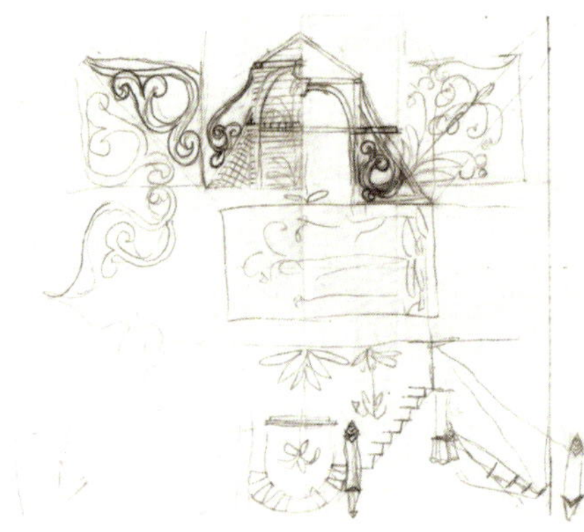

Primrose

Primula vulgaris   زهرة الربيع الشائعة

Symmetry and repetition are widely used techniques in Islamic art. Experimenting with different combinations leads to the final design.

This archetypal woodland flower is a feature of both urban and rural Britain from late February onwards, sometimes flowering well into the summer in shady spots. Roadside banks, especially those that go through woodland, are a great place to see masses of yellow primroses, but you'll need to be on a bicycle to appreciate them.

Primroses were commonly associated with clearings in woodlands. Whenever the wood was cut or a large tree fell letting sunlight reach the ground, long-dormant primroses burst into flower. Sadly, woodland management, especially coppicing, has all but died out and modern coppicing practice isn't extensive enough to let primroses flourish, which leads to a decline in the seedbank in the soil. We have to wait for great trees to fall, which is possibly even sadder than the decline in primroses.

There are scattered populations around most British towns and villages and a springtime walk in the woods is greatly enhanced by the discovery of a clump in full bloom. Churchyards often have good populations and many are now managed to encourage them.

They are, of course, the predecessors of the larger and more colourful primroses used to create bedding displays in parks and gardens.

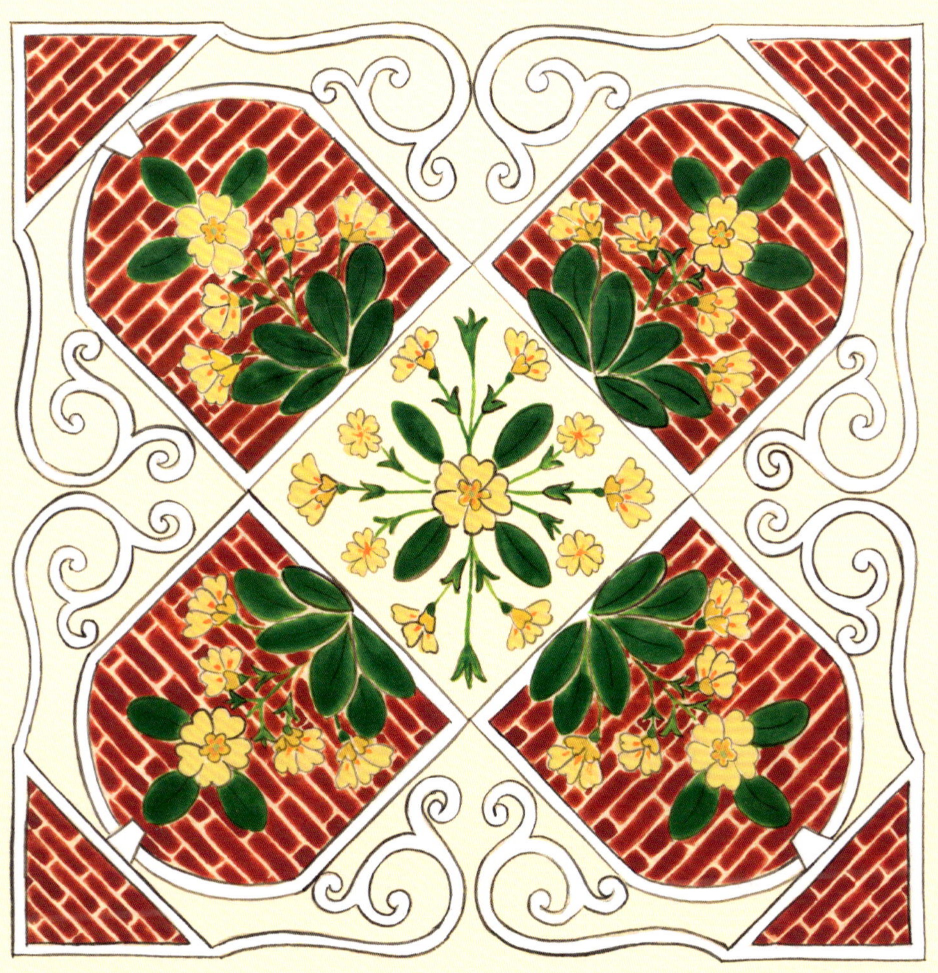

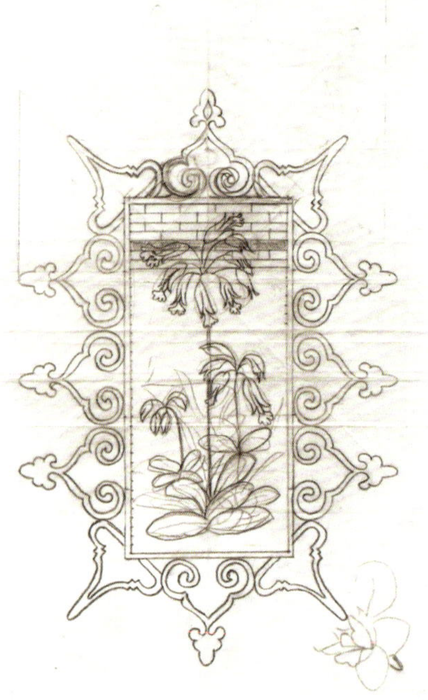

Orientation makes a difference. The landscape format of the final piece provides space to enrich the design with more flowers and details. Repetition is used to balance the flowers with the arches.

Cowslip

Primula veris

زهرة الربيع العطري

From March through to early June, the little nodding heads of cowslips are some of the most charismatic flowers of pasture, and are now, sadly, quite scarce. When the conditions are just right they do very well, but they do need to be out in full sun, unlike their shade-loving brethren the primroses. They like poor soil and not too much vigorous competition from grass. Even when seeds are sown specifically to grace a meadow, their choosy nature means they don't always take off.

Where the ground is dry and the grass is short and grazed, they can thrive. Nature reserves are often the best places to look, as the specific conditions they need don't often occur by accident any more and it takes careful management to ensure they succeed. Steep motorway banks that catch the sun can be good habitats, especially now that emissions from car exhausts are less polluting. Find a field full of them on a warm, lengthening day in early summer and you can also be assured there will be lots of bees, butterflies and crickets. They are a great indicator of a thriving ecosystem. Cowslips are always yellow and delicate but they can hybridise with primulas in built-up areas, as the pollen is carried by bees from garden to pastureland. Some amazing varieties have resulted from this cross-pollination, including the false oxlip, a primrose on a stalk.

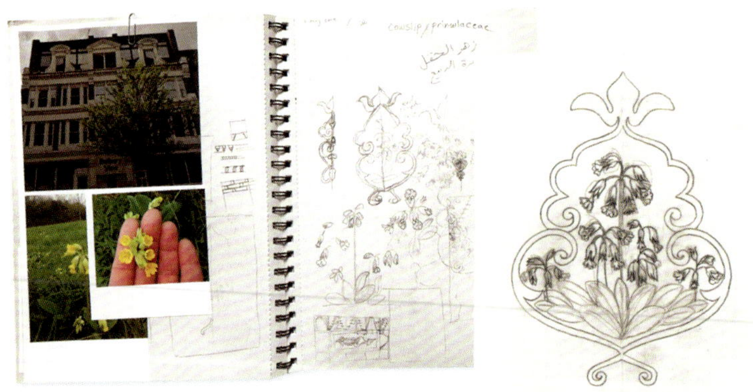

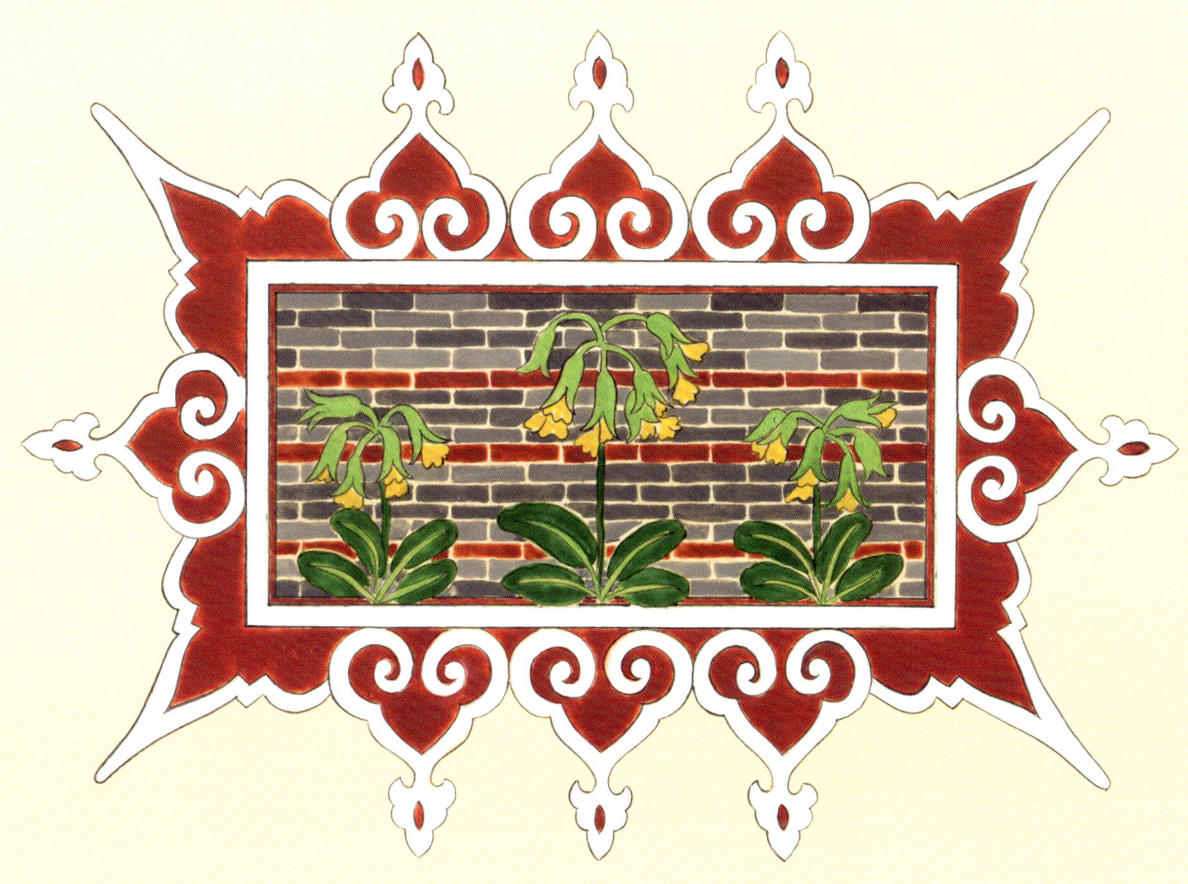

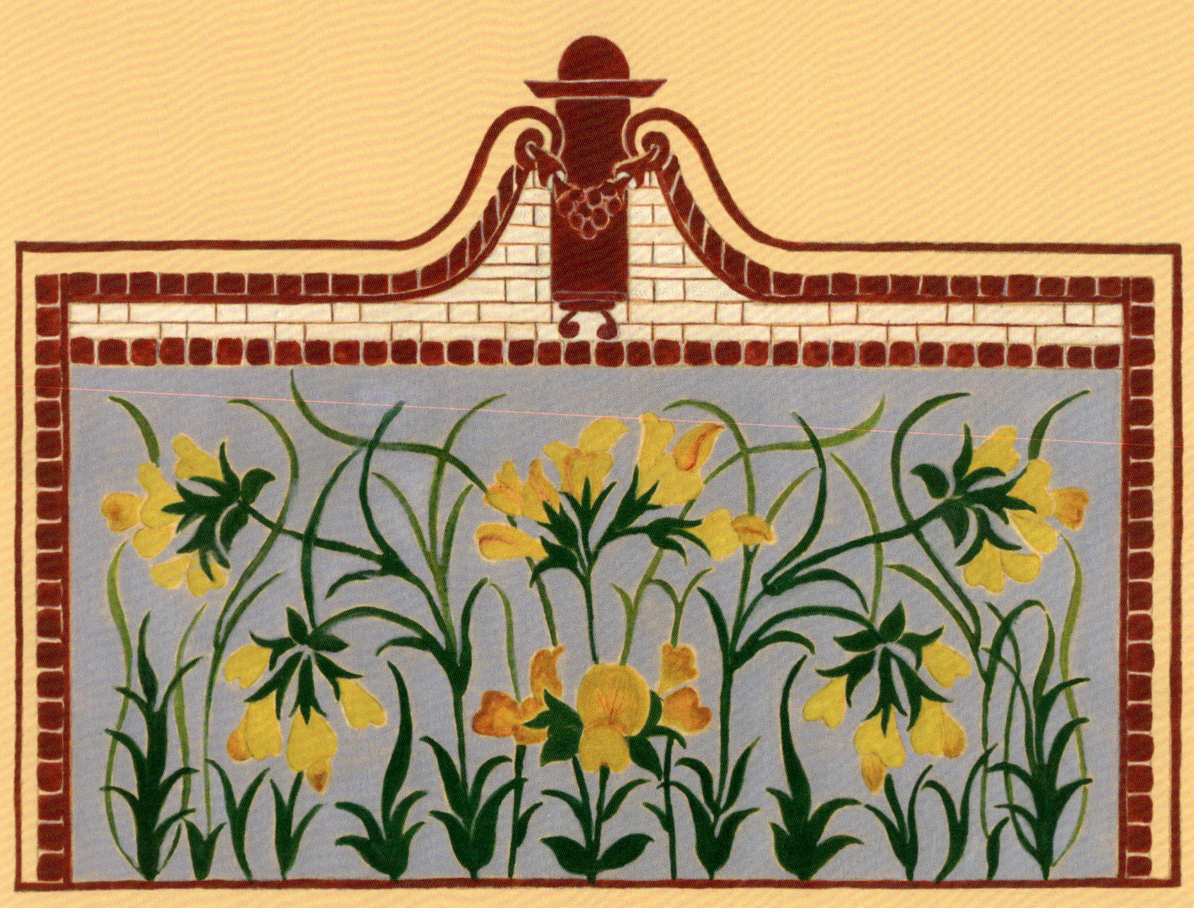

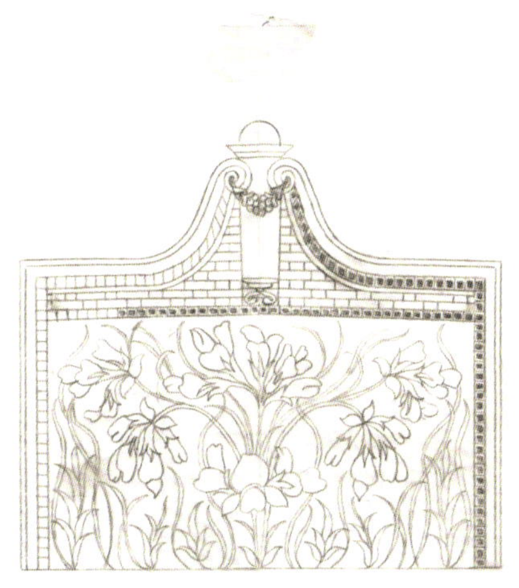

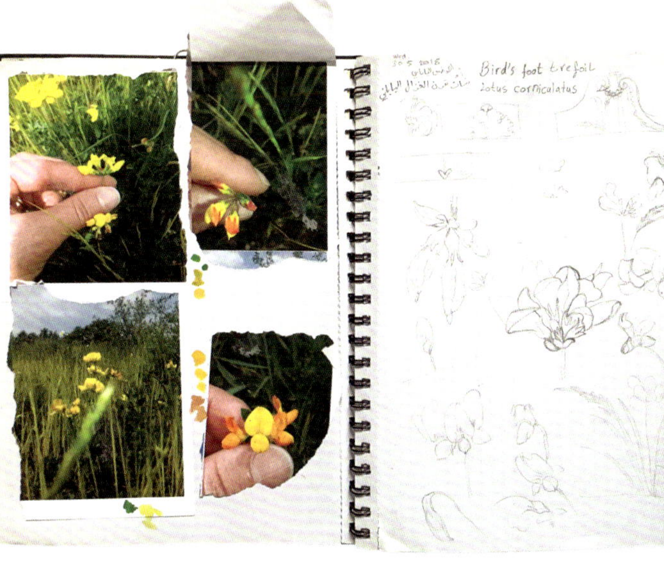

The initial abstract design for this composition had a square frame but once the layout for the flowers emerged, it made sense to extend it in order to embrace all the elements comfortably.

Bird's foot trefoil

Lotus corniculatus

قرن الغزال

This beautiful little plant flowers all summer, from June onwards, and survives well in short lawns. In late summer it can form extensive carpets of yellow tinged with red, the colour of eggs and bacon – one of its common names.

It is really a meadow flower. If it is not mown every few days it will grow quite tall and scramble through the grasses and other wildflowers. However, it is not too fussy and also thrives in very poor soils. It blooms in well-tended, unfertilised grass verges especially where a caring resident cuts the grass and collects the clippings. A verge in high summer covered in flowers is a wonderful thing and all it takes to make this joy come about is relaxing your mowing regime during the hot dry months of July and August.

Bees love bird's foot trefoil, as do many other insects that need nectar, and it often grows alongside clovers and other nectar-rich flowers. If left

Pick and mix: exploring various architectural elements and finally picking simple ones to guarantee an uncluttered design.

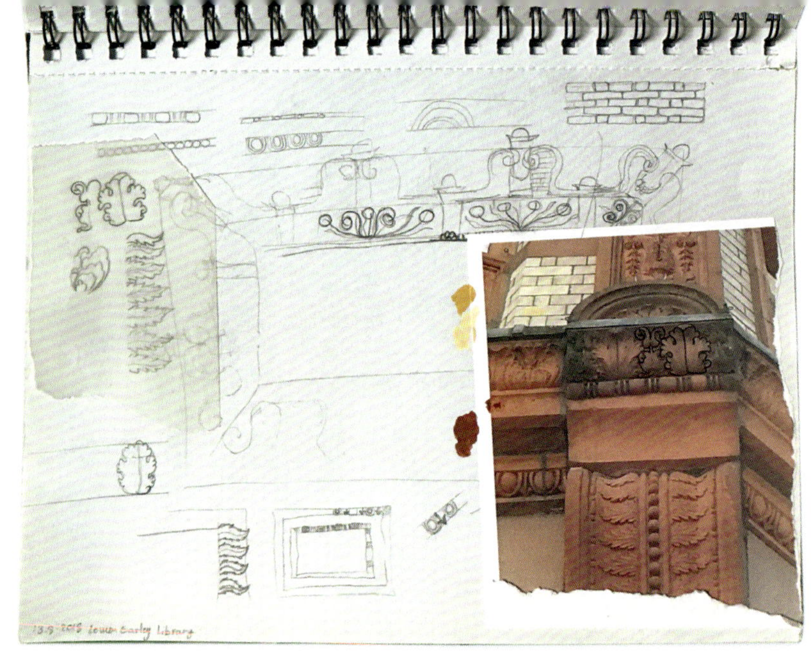

unmown for a while, goldfinches add another level of delight as they snack on the seeds.

It has a whole host of local names, some associated with the shape of the flower, which looks like a little shoe, some with the colour. The best is derived from the shape of its seed pods: Granny's toenails!

The frame for the bird's foot trefoil is based on the incredibly elaborate Edwardian brickwork of Queen Victoria Street, whose symmetry and level of detail drew Hadil's eye. A relatively new street in the history of Reading, it was built a little over a century ago to provide a direct route from the station to Broad Street. The road was the work of Councillor Fidler, a local businessman who was also responsible for acquiring Prospect Park for the town. The brickwork has clearly been influenced by the Victorian designs of the Town Hall and many of the great houses of the time. It is very easily overlooked as the lower levels are all modern shops and few people remember to look up and admire the decorative terracotta work above.

Ox-eye daisy

Leucanthemum vulgare

أقحوان المروج الشائع

There is little better than a warm sunny day in a wildflower meadow in midsummer. As butterflies flit and crickets chirp, the swaying flowers of ox-eye daisies complete the picture and as the light fades on a summer's evening, they glow luminously. They are also known as moon flowers.

From late May to late July and in many settings the flowers can take over and become rampant. They transform urban sites with abandoned derelict buildings and disturbed soils, 'waste places', but are also at home in managed meadows and parks. Although common, they do come and go mysteriously. A few years ago, Balmore Walk in Caversham had a mass of them. Recently, they have all but gone. Over the last 30 years, they

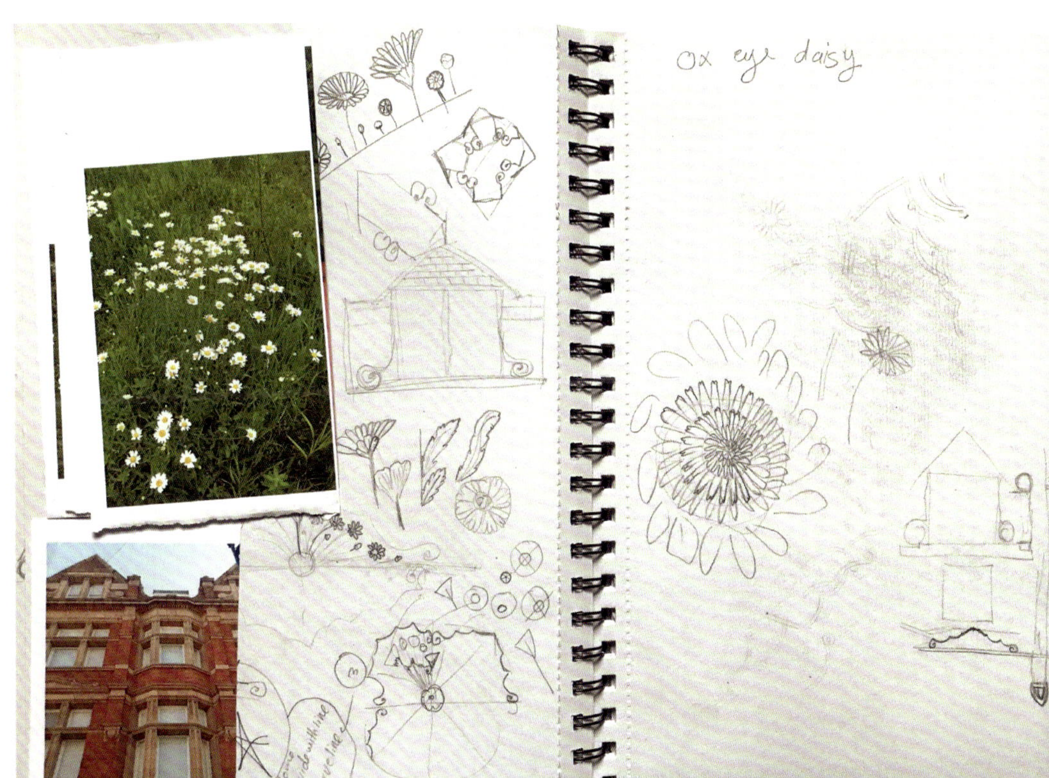

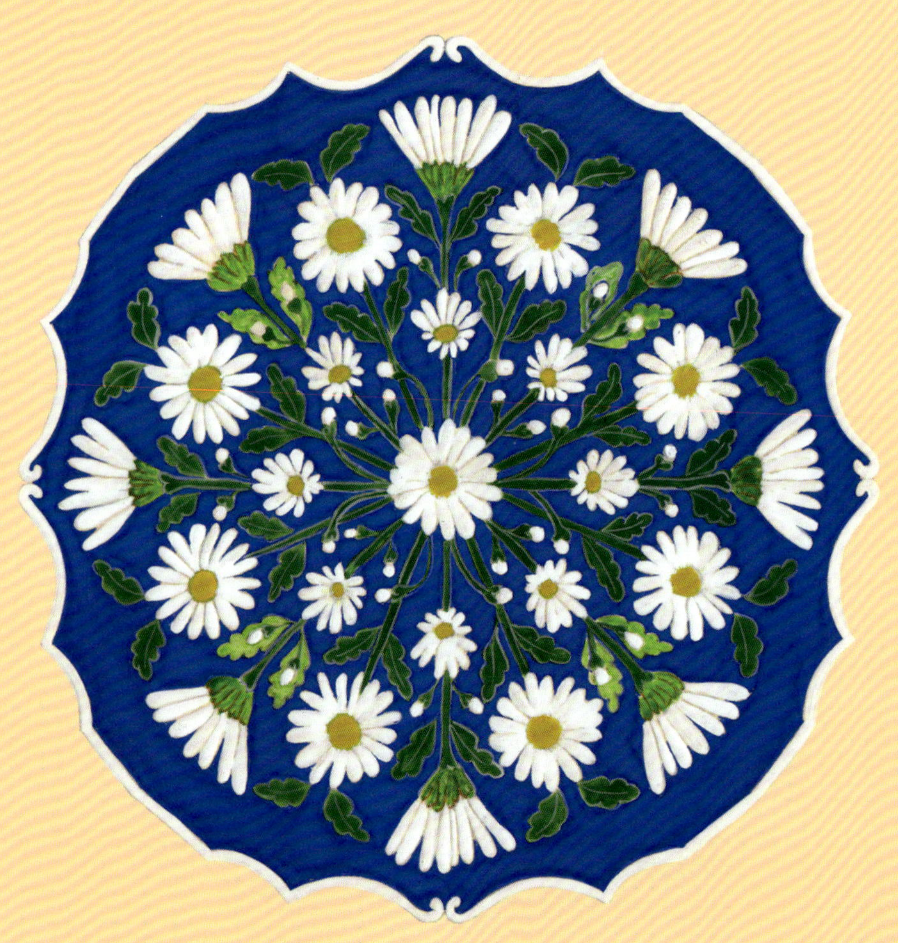

A simple flower yet a challenging design. The answer was a rounded arrangement to match the shape of the flower. For this composition, I employed geometric principles and the repetition technique.

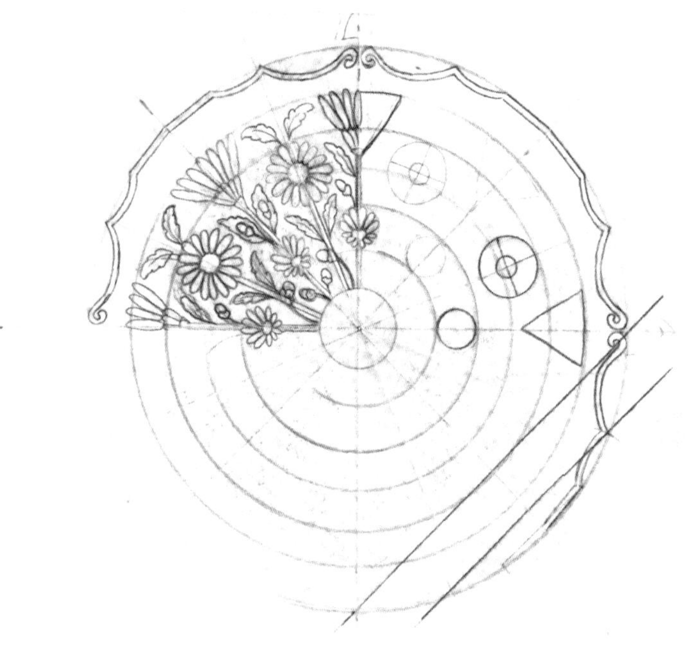

have slowly become established in the meadow in front of the mansion house in Prospect Park. One day they will form a gorgeous, summer-long throng there.

Late in the summer the ripened flower heads are easy to strip of their seeds and no one will complain if you scatter them elsewhere to spread their beauty.

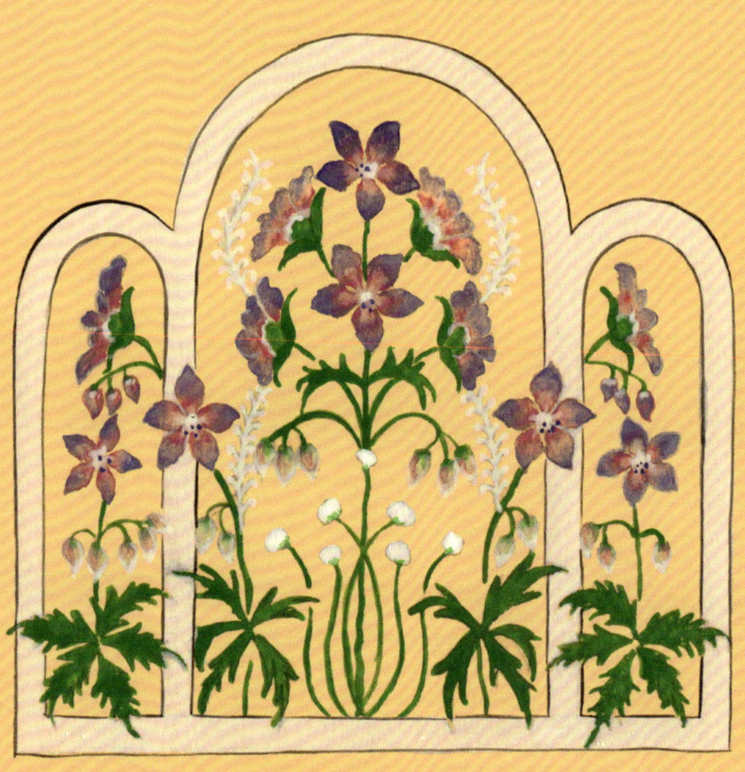

Meadow cranesbill

Geranium pratense

الغرنوقي المرجي

An inhabitant of summer hay meadows and hedgerows, this is one of many wild geraniums still common enough to find among the long grasses. The flowers appear in May and continue well into the autumn. As many meadows are now managed for the flora not the hay, their flowering season is a bit longer than it might have been in years past.

It is another superb plant for bees. The bright purple, open flowers are repeatedly visited and you can see the pollen in the baskets on the bees' legs as they carry it back to feed the colony, and, of course, make honey.

The name 'cranesbill' comes from the shape of the seed head and you need to be familiar with the common crane to note the resemblance. The birds must have been a common sight in England if the shape of their head and beak was used to name a seed head! The closely related dove's foot cranesbill combines features of two birds in its name and it's worth looking out for too.

Both plants spread their seeds by explosive force. As the seed heads dry and become taut, they suddenly burst and the seed is catapulted to pastures new.

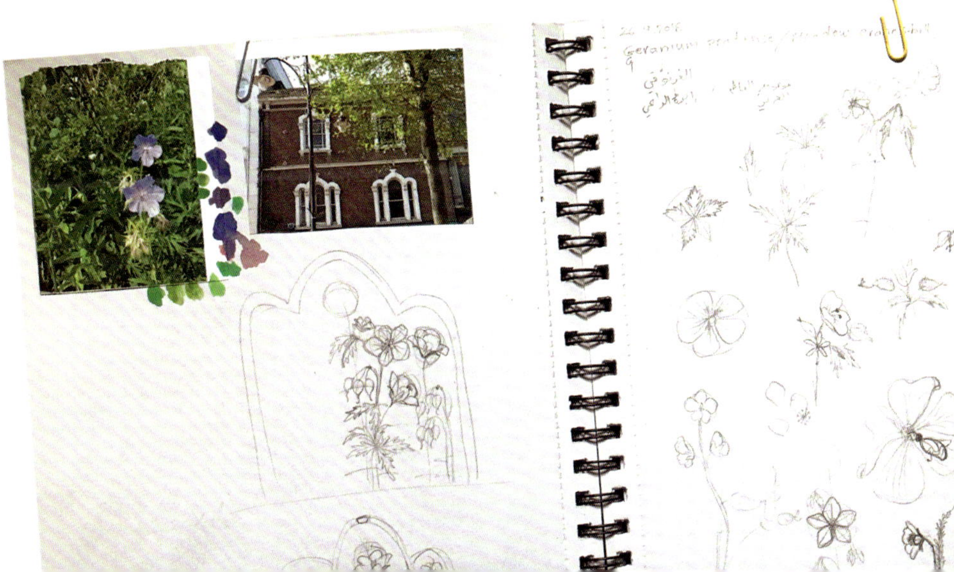

Experimentation: trial and error, developing ideas and the element of surprise at the end. The frame design matches the flower shape creating a harmonious composition.

Yellow flag iris

Iris pseudacorus

السوسن الأصفر

The yellow flag iris is a common plant along riverbanks, in wet meadows and in ditches. The tall sword-shaped leaves appear in midwinter and soon grow to dominate the wet margin. Then, in late May, the flowers appear. First just one, like a bright star appearing in the evening sky. As the days pass, more and more appear till by mid-June they are at a splendid peak. It is a wild member of the iris family, popular with gardeners, but you wouldn't want this in any but the biggest of gardens as it really is a vigorous plant. They spread via rhizomes, which helps them to dominate an area quickly, and their seeds help them to spread by germinating readily along the bankside.

The flowers produce huge amounts of nectar, more per bloom than any other wildflower. So, they attract many different insects and have an important role to play in reviving diminishing populations.

The roots have some valuable medicinal properties, not least the use of a slice on an aching tooth.

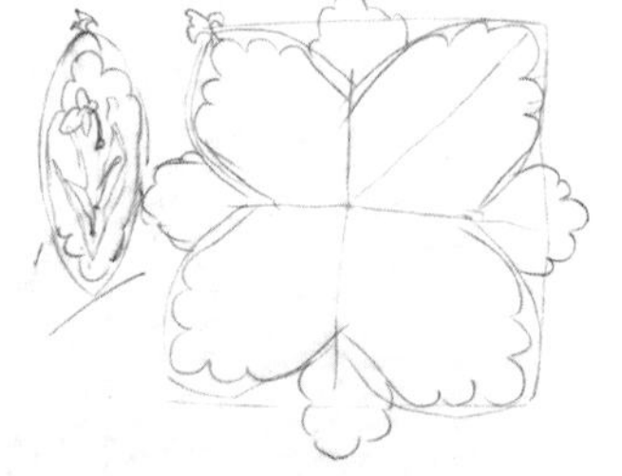

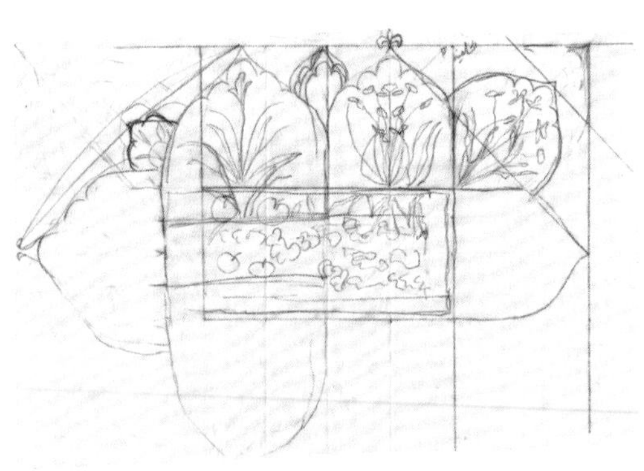

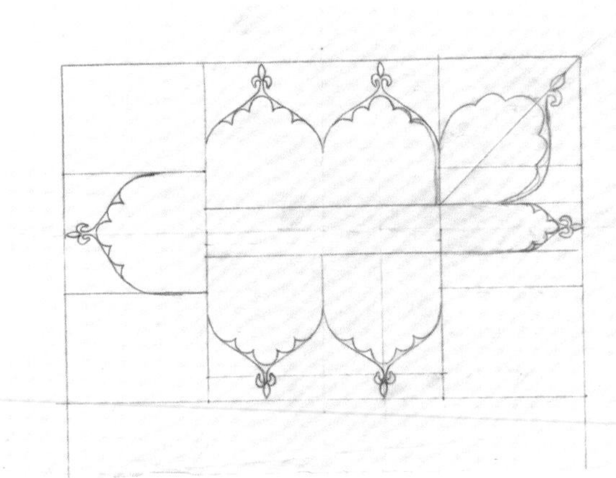

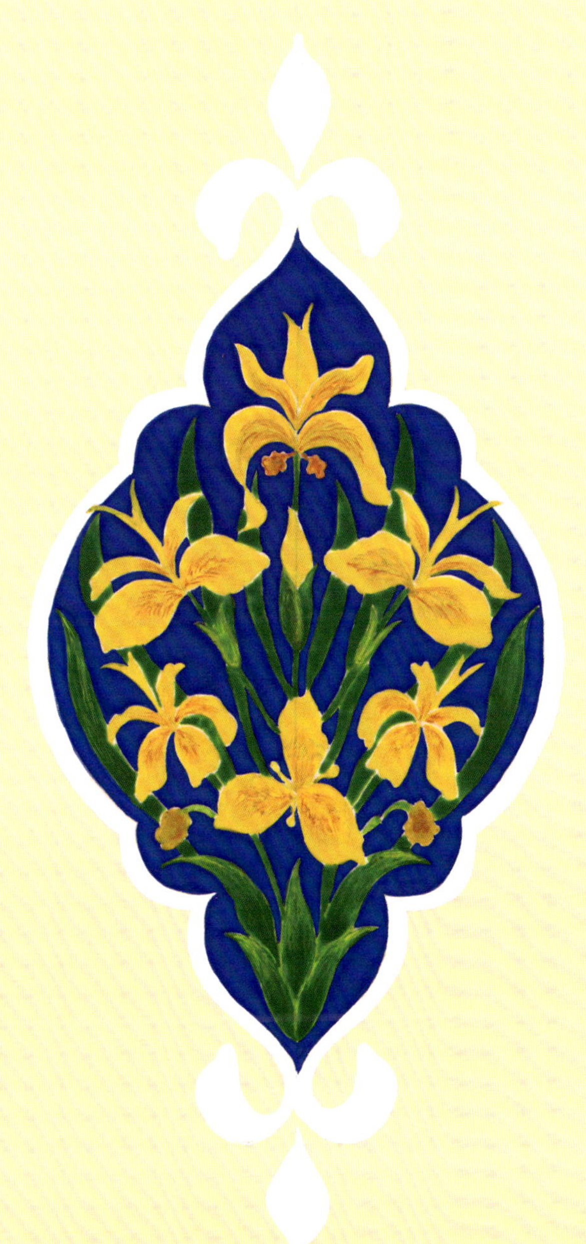

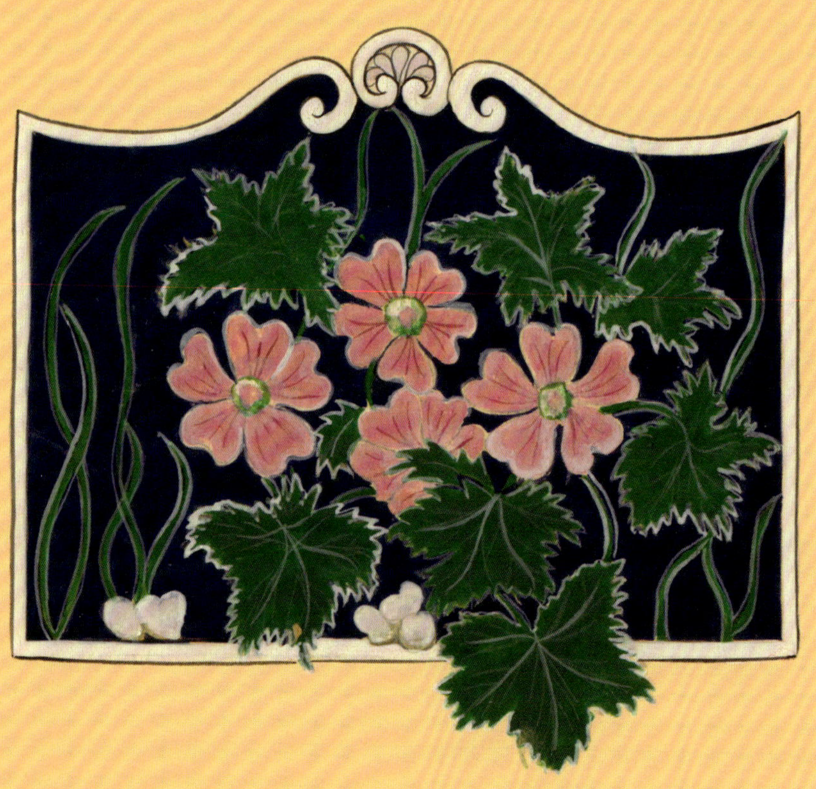

Common mallow

Malva sylvestris

الخبازة

The more relaxed mowing regimes in some of our parks, public open spaces and grass verges have been very beneficial to common mallow. Despite having large fan-shaped leaves it doesn't seem to mind being brutally cut back by the mowers and will spring up again among even the most vigorous grasses. It is one of only a few plants that can tolerate such treatment.

The dark pink flowers are large and open, another good plant for insects searching for nectar. They flower from late May, right through to the autumn. As summer wears on and the grasses start to fade, the dark green leaves stand out. The roots are deep and even drought fails to hold the plant back. It just flowers all the more.

Plenty of everything: plenty of ideas, plenty of floral details, plenty of colours, plenty of compositions.

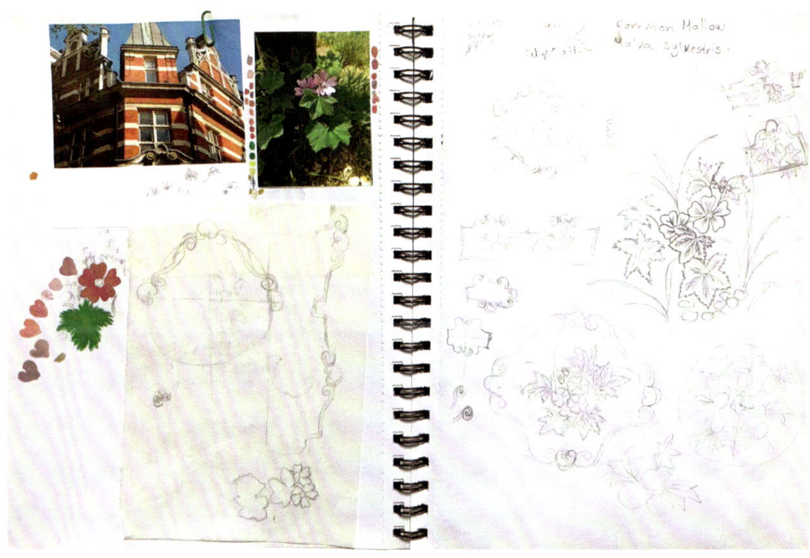

The entrance of the building inspired the frame design. Few passers-by look up to notice the decorated roof gables andturrets of the Lloyds Bank building on Broad Street. The swirls on the roof top are echoed in the doorway and, together with the roof profile, inspired the frame design for common mallow.

A truly ubiquitous plant, mallow grows across the globe and can be found at the coast and on the hillside. It doesn't seem to mind whether it grows in gravel or under hedgerows, on wasteland or meadows.

Nearly all mallows are edible and they have many medicinal uses, being high in iron, vitamins and mucilage (which can help soothe inflammation and irritation). It's a great plant for eating; the leaves can be eaten cooked or raw, but avoid plants alongside roads due to contamination from exhaust fumes and avoid picking from places dogs may visit. Perhaps collect some seeds and grow them in the safe environment of your own garden. The round seedpods provided snacks for children on their way home from school in days past – they were called 'cheeses'.

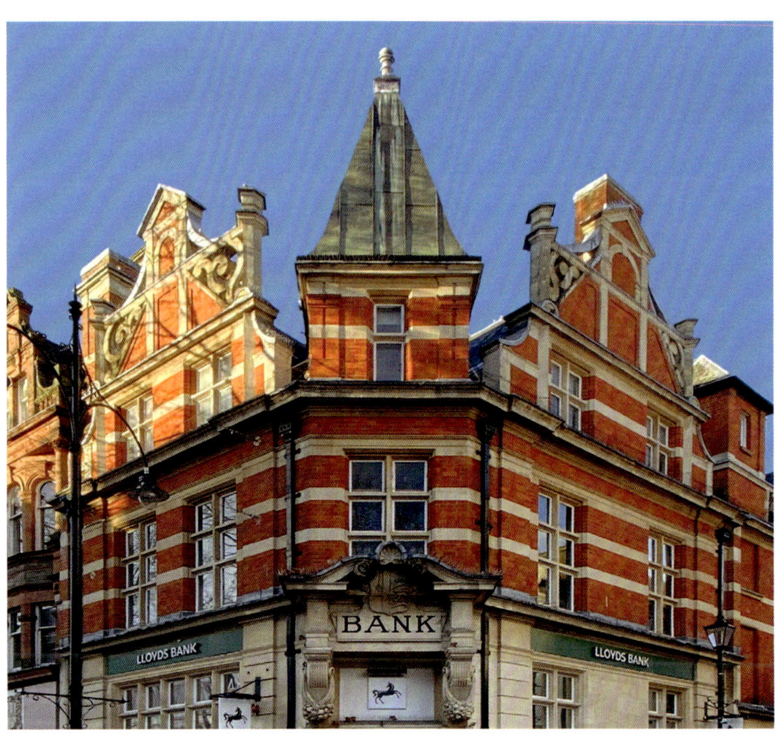

A tall and vigorous plant like comfrey deserves a tall, stepped frame inspired by the architecture of the distinguished building at 120 Broad Street.

Comfrey

Symphytum officinale

الشاغة المخزنية

Comfrey, renowned for its health-giving properties, is abundant in damp, out-of-the-way places. It has a preference for some shade so can be found at the edge of wet woodlands, the edges of marshes and along canal sides. The plant comes into growth quite early in the year, flowering as soon as the weather is warm enough, and keeps going until the first frost.

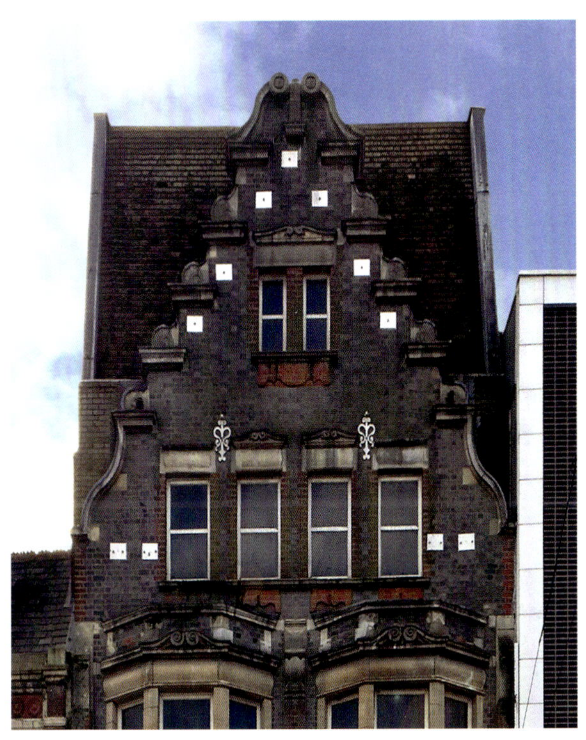

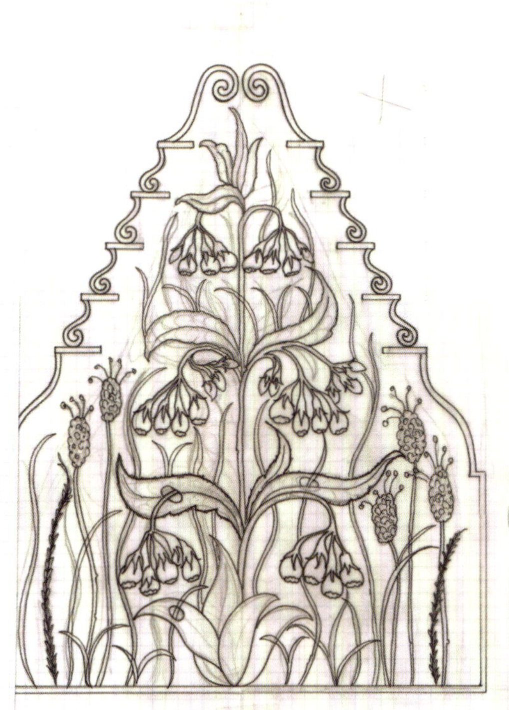

The flowers hang in little bunches, often nodding as bees crawl in and out. They are incredible producers of nectar and vary in colour from a pale pinkish white, through pink itself, to purple. By midsummer plants can look jaded and rough though. Caterpillars and slugs have munched through the leaves, the stems snap in the wind, or they get trampled. However, cut them back and they grow back lush and vigorous, almost begging to be cut again.

It's a fairly tall and vigorous plant, probably not well suited to a small garden as it can take over. There are various differently coloured garden varieties which are more controllable. The hairy leaves (which can irritate the skin) make a superb fertiliser when soaked in water and allowed to rot down, especially for things growing in pots.

Comfrey has a huge list of common names but the often-used one, Knitbone, refers to its healing properties. A poultice can be made from the fleshy leaves and roots and is apparently miraculous. Traditionally, a 'tea' was made from the leaves to soothe aches and pains but safety concerns about some of the chemicals it contains mean it is not recommended that you drink any.

Comfrey's ability to rejuvenate means that in late September and, these days, even into October the plants cut earlier in the year flower again and provide valuable autumn nectar for the bees, while the uncut plants are sprawling masses of tatty leaves and seed heads.

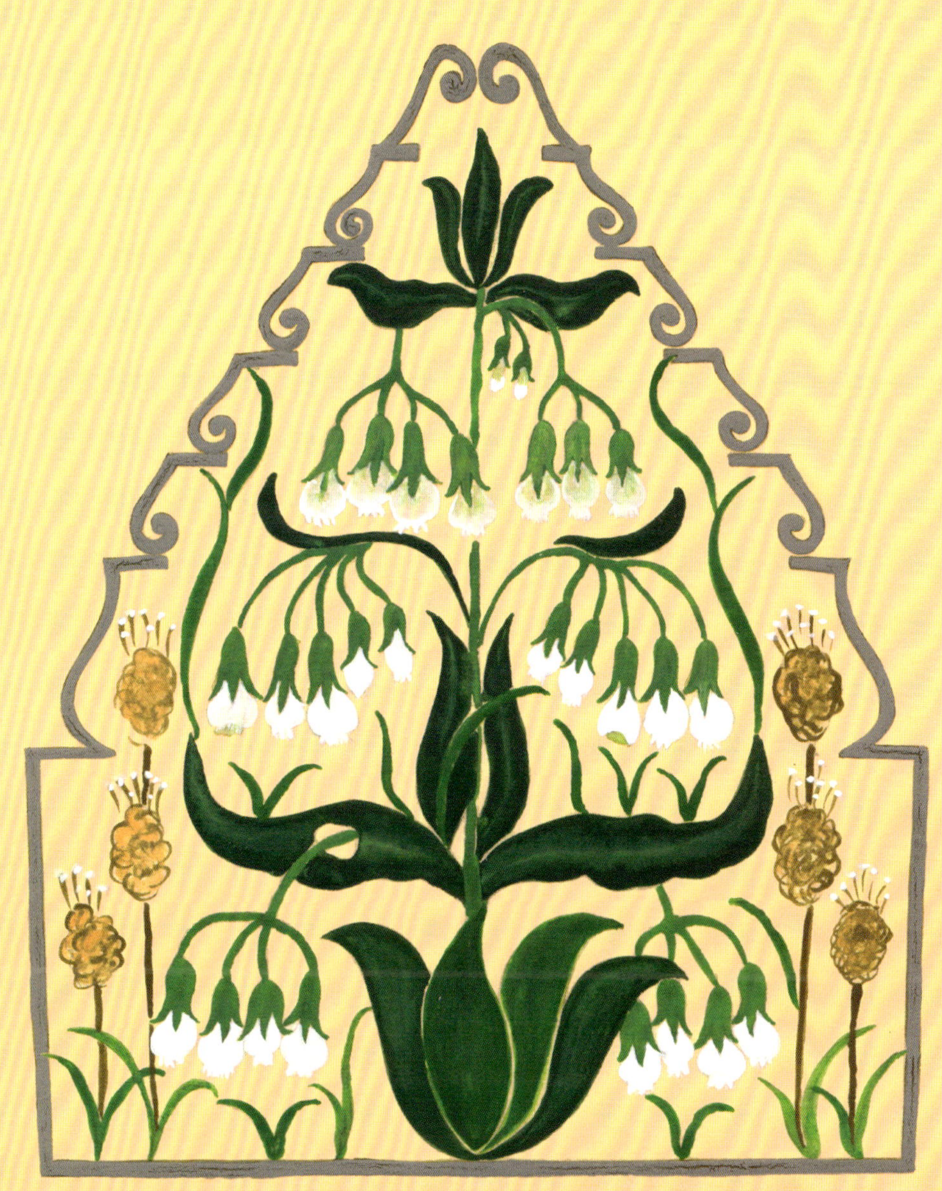

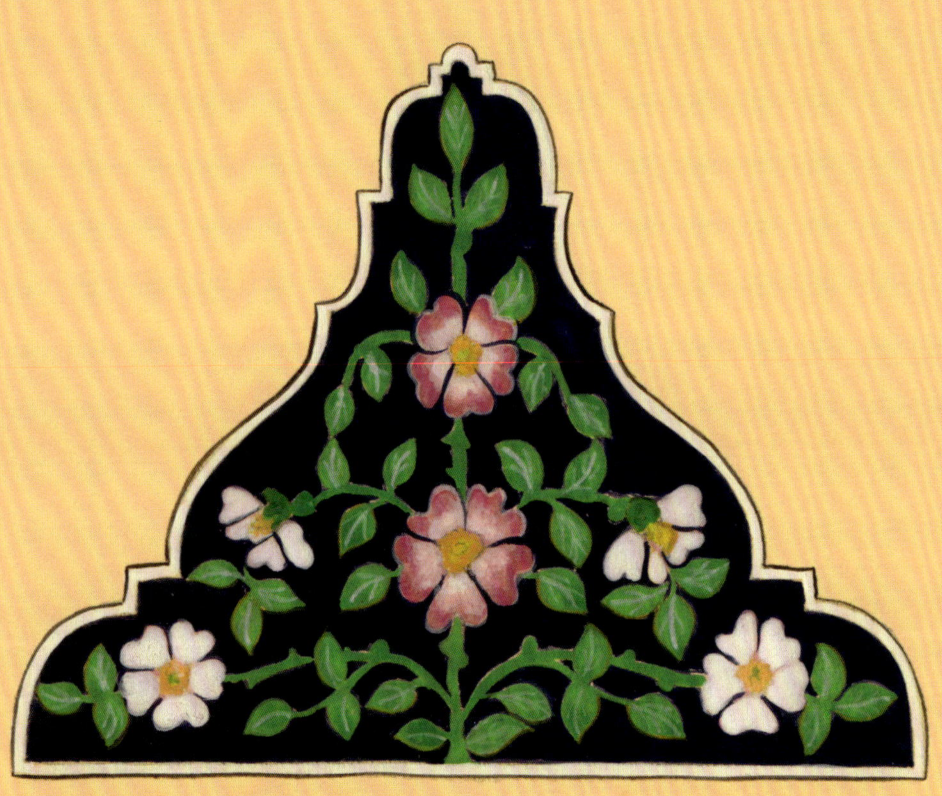

Wild or dog rose

Rosa canina

النسرين

The delicate pink shades of wild roses can be found all over the countryside from May onwards, although they are not so easy to find in towns. They grow alongside paths and hedgerows, the edges of woodlands and often with bramble thickets and in among hawthorn bushes.

The beautiful, simple flowers, wide open and slightly aromatic, are abundant in high summer and fill the bushes and hedgerows at a time of year when almost all the other flowers are beginning to fade. The hawthorn, blackthorn and bramble are all in full leaf, their fruits are beginning to form and often the only flower left in the hedgerows is the wild rose. Not only do they add colour and beauty, they provide pollen and nectar, so they are always busy with life. Once the summer is past,

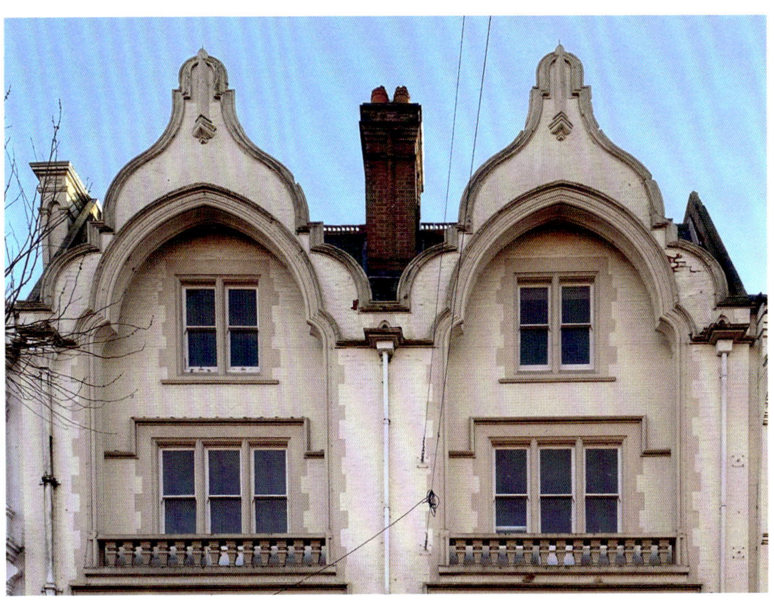

the fruits add their own beauty to the hedgerow as the leaves fall. The vicious thorns on the long straggling stems are cleverly designed; as the winter winds blow they act like a ratchet so the stems are blown one way but can't spring back again, enabling them to spread over paths and hedges.

There are several different species. The most common is the dog rose. The smaller, less thorny field rose is less pink, more typically white, and is altogether a more delicate plant.

The fruits, bright red barrel-shaped hips, attract many birds and small mammals and are terrifically good for you, full of lovely vitamins and essential fats. Rose hip syrup was a staple in the past, as it is an excellent source of vitamin C. Nowadays the hips are frequently collected for home-made tonics.

Bramble

Rubus fruticosus

العليق

Bramble is notorious for its straggling stems and vicious thorns, and famous for its delicious fruit freely available all summer long. It is less well known for its flowers, which are bright white and full of pollen, contrasting beautifully with the dark green leaves. They do warrant close examination should you get the chance.

Bramble grows anywhere that has been abandoned to nature. It's the most common flowering plant in Britain. Sprouting readily from seed dropped by birds, badgers and foxes that have feasted on the fruits, it colonises woodlands under the shade of the trees and along footpaths,

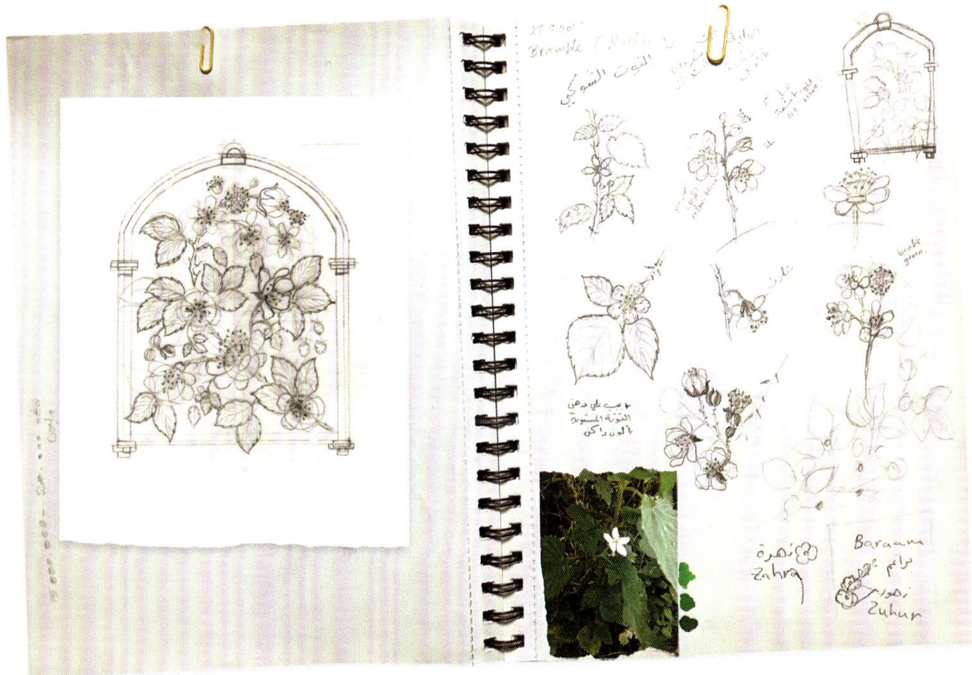

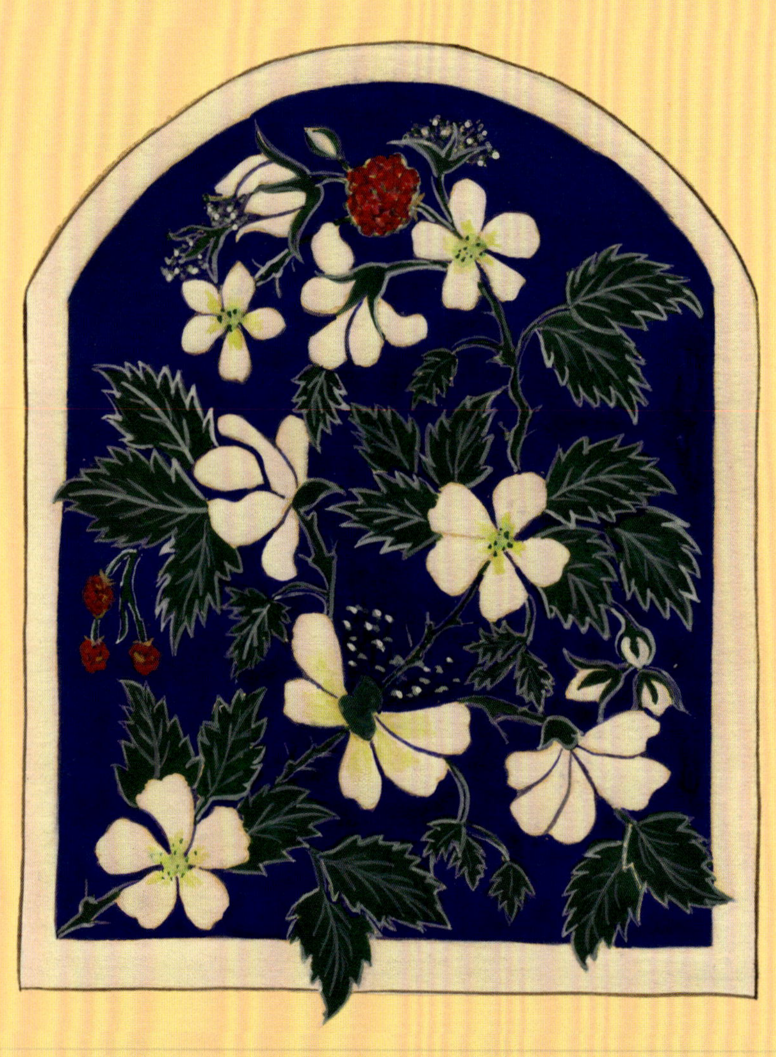

where it snags the unwary. Nature's barbed wire, it is very effective at keeping browsing animals away and acts as a protector to seedling trees.

Undervalued these days despite its generosity with fruit, bramble's vigorous growth habit helps to reclaim land for nature, swarming with insects all summer long, home to countless nesting birds and timid mammals. The arching stems grow at a prodigious rate, rooting where they touch the ground and soon taking over. But it does not take long for sapling trees to grow from beneath it and then shade it out.

As long as you're wearing protective clothing, a stand of brambles rewards the explorer. Look for old bird nests in the winter, bees on the flowers in spring and juicy fruit in the summer.

Don't Apologise for What You Have Done

By Mahmoud Darwish

Here all of your memories are visible:
Midday ennui in a cat somnolence,
the cockscomb,
a scent of sage,
mother's coffee,
a straw mat with pillows,

لا تعتذرْ عمَّا فَعَلْتَ

محمود درويش

ها هِيَ ذكرياتُكَ كُلُّها مرئيَّةٌ:
ضَجَرُ الظهيرة في نُعَاس القطِّ
عُرْف الديكِ
عطرُ المريميَّةِ
قهوةُ الأمِّ
الحصيرةُ والوسائدُ

Thanks to the NHS

This wonderful and unique artwork was specially designed and created by Hadil in Spring 2020 to say thank you to the NHS for their sacrificial commitment to their work during the COVID-19 pandemic. The resulting lockdown delayed publication of this book which was originally planned for June 2020. Hadil uses her art to build bridges in complex and difficult situations. This book is her creative response to the conflict that exists between her two homes, England and Palestine and, in the same vein, the design below is a gift of beauty to counter the destructive and heart-breaking power of the virus.

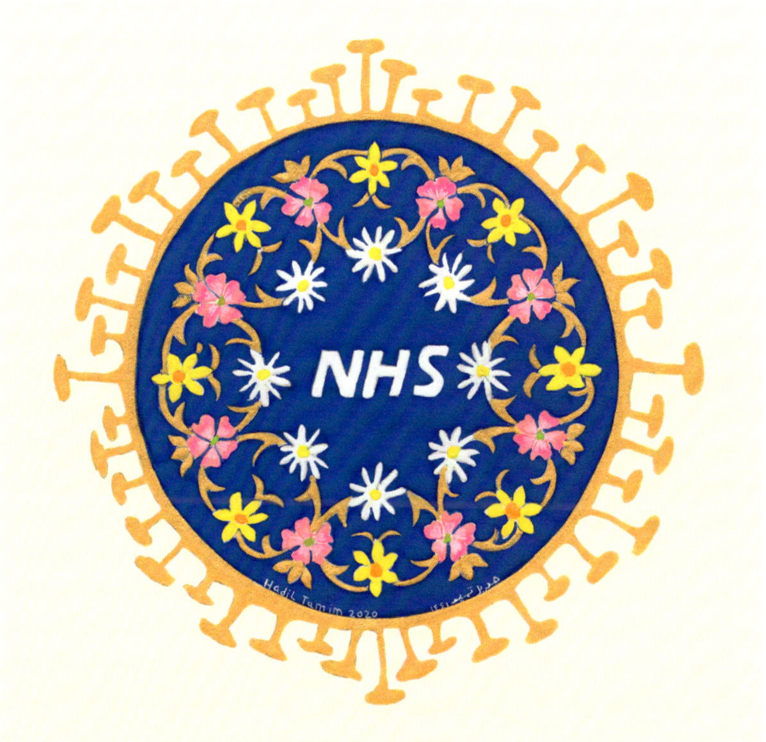

Thank you NHS for all your endless efforts during these difficult times.

Two Rivers Press has been publishing in and about Reading
since 1994. Founded by the artist Peter Hay (1951–2003), the press
continues to delight readers, local and further afield, with its varied list
of individually designed, thought-provoking books.

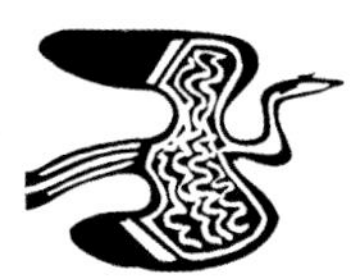